Electronic cities
&
Web-based urbanization integrated systems

Electronic cities
&
Web-based urbanization integrated systems

Develop & create a master plan, implement & build a sample

MARYAM KAMRANI
AND
AMIR ALIKHANZADEH

iUniverse, Inc.
New York Lincoln Shanghai

Electronic cities & Web-based urbanization integrated systems
Develop & create a master plan, implement & build a sample

iUniverse books may be ordered through booksellers or by contacting:

iUniverse
2021 Pine Lake Road, Suite 100
Lincoln, NE 68512
www.iuniverse.com
1-800-Authors (1-800-288-4677)

ISBN: 978-0-595-45738-0 (pbk)
ISBN: 978-0-595-69833-2 (cloth)
ISBN: 978-0-595-90040-4 (ebk)

Printed in the United States of America

To our son Amirhessam, the first great love of our life, and to all of those who followed.

CONTENTS

LIST OF TABLES

LIST OF FIGURES

ABOUT THE BOOK

Imagine after getting your pilot's license for flying small, single-engine airplanes, you traveled from LA to NY on a Boeing 747. Looking out the window at those perfectly circular irrigated farms in Nebraska and Iowa, my lazy thoughts drifted from corn to water to football to rope swings splashing into Summer Rivers. There was a small airport below. Would that make a good emergency field? What if this plane had an emergency? What if we were on autopilot and a flight attendant interrupted the movie to ask if there were a pilot on board? I know that if I had to sit in the left seat of that 747, I wouldn't have a clue, and the plane would go down. I wouldn't know what to make of thousands of switches, glass screens, levers, pedals, blinking lights, and somewhere a radio. It's like that when you learn how to implement an electronic city. Those sinking feelings. That frustration. That not knowing. But because you have this book in hand, you are already in the pilot's seat and on the learning curve. Relax; step by step it will get easier. In the same way tens of thousands of pilots have learned to fly, you will learn to make and implement or at least live in an electronic city. Once man, machine and money were the most important resources in an organization but now information is also one of the most important factors and in fact after man it is the most important resource in an organization. Companies have come to this agreement that in order to controlling and monitoring the costs of establishing management information systems by computer they need new paths, policies and executive methods. The master plan of an e-city is a powerful tool which is interested in developing the existing technology, creating information interaction among organizations and citizens that finally moves toward integrating with the e-city development plan.

PART ONE

An electronic city

PREFACE

The master plan of an e-city is a powerful tool which is interested in developing the existing technology, creating information interaction among organizations and citizens that finally moves toward integrating with the e-city development plan.

Our focus in this book is far from details and is based on Russell Ackoff theory. Means it is totally organizational and far from execution which will coordinate all the IT development activities toward better urban services, so it will prevent all parallel or opposed activities in an electronic city.

Once man, machine and money were the most important resources in an organization but now information is also one of the most important factors and in fact after man it is the most important resource in an organization. Companies have come to this agreement that in order to controlling and monitoring the costs of establishing management information systems by computer they need new paths, policies and executive methods.

Municipalities are also some of these organizations and in order to make accurate and on time decisions and being aware of situation at any moment, they need automation systems in their organizations.

Municipalities are actually of those types of organizations that faces a lot of changes in their policies environment and are continuously experiencing the new methods which changes the way of the staffs' tasks so, database oriented systems that are going to be designed for them should be flexible according to the changes they face. In such environment that is always experiencing changes, the policy makers' needs may change daily so, in order to answering the management requests accurate, flexible and reliable a powerful MIS is needed. Right now most of the municipalities face the lack of proper management information system or the improper ones.

As an example in most of the municipalities in a country like Iran the real estates auditing systems are not integrated and they are like isolated islands. These information systems store the information gathered by physical observation of the real estates in the shape of files and records then by using special indexes they convert the real estates' characteristics to the estimated cost and finally the output will be the price of the building and based on it the tax will

1

be accounted and printed. When there are mass of such repetitive tasks these systems seems helpful in increasing the efficiency but today most of the organizations needs some how the same information and it is unwise and costly to provide the same information repeatedly.

The importance of information transaction shows itself in such situations. Information must not be limited by any organization. In other words managers are aware of the importance of shared information nowadays. This awareness has caused to the request for integrated systems. In an integrated system, information can be shared among different parts of the organization fast and easy by a database administration. It seems the core of an MIS design is in the heart of a DBA (the possibility of accessing to all information needs is important to the existence and efficiency of any organization). This by itself will cease to DBs reduction into one or two total ones. Global looking when designing these databases provides the possibility of information logical concatenation from different resources. Through such a vision the designing of integrated systems especially urbanization integrated system based on the municipality of Mashed will be discussed in this book in 3 levels namely: functional, management and policies information in which the pyramid of municipality information has been in the center of consideration.

M.Kamrani
A.Alilkhanzadeh

Chapter 1

INTRODUCTION

Information and information dissemination is almost the most important strategic tools for management and accurate managing of all the economic, social, cultural and political units. Based on the depth and complexity of economic, cultural, social and political relations and situations cities are put in different priorities in a country.

Considering the importance of information, IT tools and methods are developing very fast in today's world. It has affected all aspects of human activities.

As mentioned IT is growing so fast especially in the field of urban life. Electronic cities provide software, hardware and necessary infrastructure and platforms which are needed for easy access ability of citizens to official and non-official databases 24/7 on web. Electronic municipalities' mission is moving toward becoming citizen oriented, so people can get a large amount of their urban services while they are at home which will cease in traffic reduction, better services fast and qualified with normal price from anywhere anytime.

Urban management can act better in e-cities because of the interactions between different urban parts and the existence of value systems. Actually e-cities and municipalities are created in 4 steps or phases: establishing, upgrading, interacting and integrating.

The first step is producing a strategic plan for creating an e-city according to the feasibility study of the existing situation, coordinating, customizing and adapting and adjusting these programs with similar ones in the world. Most of e-cities and municipalities have started with web-sites and has focused on training on the next phase. In the third step portals are developed and people can interact with e-municipalities easily and here after e-banking will be available for people. Through implementing the integrating phase most of the urban services are accessible and people can benefit the city services through internet, at this stage an e-municipality has been formed and stabled. Some of the best e-cities prototypes like Berlin and Toronto are classified in this category.

Creating virtual organization and implementing Tele-working are the future programs of the cities of this kind.

Mashed as the second metropolis in Iran is candidate as one of the four pilots for implementing IT plans in the country. The city potentials like more than 13 million tourists a year, economic opportunities for investment, industrial infrastructures, long boarders with CIS countries, tens of universities and many other factors has attracted the especial attention in selecting it as an e-city pilot in this book.

1-1 Problem definition

In the third millennium, IT has been recognized as the most important axis toward the world development. IT is so mixed in the peoples' lives that a little less attention will cause big trouble. The existence of e-city and internet city as a sample in a country can be counted as a good background for the logical, stage-by-stage, practical and scientific—economic IT presence there. Studies and professional surveys and actions toward developing IT in the world have proved that individual actions were generally unsuccessful so, most of the developed countries are following IT projects through public applications and integrated systems like e-cities and e-municipalities.

In developing countries IT developments and researches are very important from the CEO's point of views. Implementing national e-commerce projects, e-banking and the related rules and regulations will make a suitable infrastructure for new economic development (digital economy) and changing the existing culture.

The attempt is to reduce the digital gap between them and other countries in this field. Electronic learning has created a proper opportunity for the developing countries to use the world experiences. As mentioned before and based on what has been said lately the role of ministry of higher education, department of trade and commerce, department of education in versatility with responsibilities and traditional duties with new responsibilities and the role of ICT ministry in providing suitable communication infrastructures and producing necessary software and lower price services which are comparable in the world and will be distributed by municipalities, is very important. Of course other governmental and non-governmental organizations can be great affect in developing IT activities in parallel with their goals. The result of such integration will cease in offering better services both on functional and security aspects to the citizens.

Each country based on its economic, social and cultural situation follows specific objectives, in some fields they are different with each other but basically they follow a lot of common objectives. Accessing a suitable economic development, upgrading urban management, implementing the city master plan, improving the quality of services, improving the life cycle standards and protecting the cultural authentication, citizen's partnership in the urban activities, nutrition knowledge oriented society, proposing municipality services 24/7 are all some of the common objectives in different e-cities. Developing service facilities in cultural, educational, technical and business aspects equally for all the citizens are also some of the other common objectives of e-cities all around the world.

1-2 Significance and feasibility

e-city of Mashed with the vision of "citizen oriented" in urban management, accessing the city services 24/7, upgrading municipalities organizations in order to performing better services has been an important resource for derivation of missions, policies and applicable designs.

The reason for selecting Mashed as a pilot plan for implementing an e-city is already mentioned in brief, for example the city potentials like more than 13 million tourists and pilgrims a year, economic opportunities for investment, commercial and industrial relations with CIS countries and tens of universities, etc.

Quantity and quality of implementing an e-city is just possible through a well-down, accurate and logical master plan. In fact this strategic master plan will set the strategies, policies and plans in a way that it can satisfy the interests of the citizens and urban managers. By studying the position of IT applications in Mashed we will find out that the current situation is not comparable with the world's standards, but the new governmental facilities during the past 2 years has improved the idea of IT development in Khorasan. Mashed is the second priority of the country in this field with 37 E 1 ports and fast accessibility to a wide band by using DWDN network. Based on the mentioned equipments and the potential of the city itself, establishing the e-city of Mashed is not only possible but it is a necessity for improving the quality of life in the country.

1-3 Defining the purposes of the master plan of e-city of Mashed as a sample

This project follows some very important economical, political, cultural and social objectives. From the economical point of views developing EC, e-banking, promotion e-cards, reducing bureaucracy and cost of services, preparing a suitable field for internal and external investing are some of the objectives; from the point of social views the accessibility of citizens and tourists to the on-line services, increasing the index of satisfaction, establishing social on-line groups, e-democracy and voting and citizen's partnership in urban decisions are some of the objectives, from the point of cultural views implementing the e-city of Mashed follows these objectives; clarification, information dissemination, virtual learning, publishing e-journals and magazines, e-libraries, updating the city portal, on-line, pilgrimage and virtual museums; from the political point of view e-city project will introduce the city to the world and will upgrade the political face of the city toward a modern pioneer city in the south eastern part of Asia.

1-4 About the master plan of e-city of Mashed

This program is a tool for transferring the city toward the idealistic situation. This master plan is far from details and is whole organizational and far from execution.

It tries to coordinate all the proper activities needed in an e-city in the field of performing services for the citizens and will prohibit the parallel or opposite activities which are against the vision of the city. All countries that have been successful in implementing e-cities are indebted with their master plan as one of the primary movements in the development programs.

1-5 Presenting the proper model for creating the master plan for electronic city of Mashed

The proper and practical model in codification the e-city of Mashed master plan is benchmarked from the existing models in the world and is customized considering the city conditions, of course the basic models which are performed in the national ICT master plan and TAKFA plan has been seen and used in this prototype master plan.

In some countries the municipalities' duties are so wide that has made them to start the e-government from their municipalities. Some of the cities in the world are some how similar with Iranian cities, they have many things in common so, not only the positive points of high level e-cities but the structure of them can be benchmarked.

Chapter 2

FOUNDATION AND
BACKGROUND

2-1 View foundations

In this chapter the foundation and background of e-cities and services are discussed.

2-1-1 Background

In this part the activities of developed countries who are concerned with e-government will be mentioned and it will continue with describing Iran's activities in the field of e-government and e-cities.

2-1-1-1 e-government and e-city background in the world

The first macro step in creating an e-government in the world belongs to Singapore's IT master plan in 1992. In 1993, the U.S. national infrastructure development project based on ICT structure was done. At the same year South Korea presented her ICT infrastructure master plan. Some countries like Japan, Thailand, and England followed similar plans between 1993—1996. There is not an exact date on creating e-cities but it can be claimed that its history goes back to the first macro steps toward e-governments. In less than a decade many of e-cities have been created in the world like Berlin, Boston, Toronto and Dubai.

2-1-1-2 e-government and e-city background in Iran

In the recent years some scattered but wide activities have been done on IT by universities and different industrial training centers. The first organized programs in this field go to the spring of 2002, which named TAKFA.

On may 2001 the university of Elm-0-Sanat and the trade point of Kish together presented an IT conference which became a new rubric on IT development path, during the conference concepts and dimensions of IT like EC, e-government, e-learning, e-banking, e-card, internet and IT applications seriously and for the first time were considered. It was a very effective conference in promoting IT in the society. Following this conference some seminars and exhibitions were held which finally ceased to codification TAKFA on the next year. On July 6th 2002 based on the suggestion of Management and Planning Organization, the country's bureau council approved the necessity of research plan on electronic commerce and at the end of that year the draft of ICT master plan was presented by the ministry of ITC. Table (2-1) shows the history of IT and e-government in Iran.

Development national ICT document	2003
IT international conference in Shiraz	2002
e-government research plan	2002
IT application development plan	2002
The role of IT in occupation	2001
The world internet cities conference	2001

Table (2-1): The history of IT and e-government in Iran

2-2 Definitions

In this part the definitions of e-government, e-city, e-municipality and e-citizen will be explained and at the end of this part the scheme of the relations among the above items will be shown.

2-3 e-government

As mentioned, developing IT during the past years leaded to a wide range of activities toward implementing and developing e-government. The widespread meaning of this concept ceased in performing different type of definitions. Each definition covers just one or two of the e-government dimensions. Defining a unique definition which holds all dimensions is almost impossible. Some of the best definitions are as follows:

1-Accessing the city services through internet

2-Connecting suppliers and customers through governmental and non-governmental organizations over the internet.

3-Optimizing governmental activities through IT and digital technology

4-Accessing governmental services 24/7

Although they are not the same but they follow a unique goal that is altering the structures and official and non-official processes by using IT potentials and capabilities. E-government is not supposed to be a solution for bureaucratic problems in the official governmental system but it is considered to be a new system in managing the country which clarifies a new vision in the field of citizenship.

Since e-governments are citizen oriented or it is better to say they are customer oriented all the activities in this field are toward solving people's problems and needs. The core philosophy of a government for serving citizens will be formed in e-government, in other words e-government means:

* Serving all governmental services to the citizens 24/7

2-4 e-city

Toronto describes e-city as follows:

Electronic accessibility to the municipality and urban departments 24/7 in a sustainable, reliable, secure and confidential way.

The above definition requires an accurate and clear direction for the future so, vision and executive strategies must be defined to reach the goals. A management structure to guarantee the priorities and decisions is also necessary; now let's define e-city based on the surveys and studies: Electronic accessibility of the citizens to the municipality and urban departments and services 24/7 in a sustainable, secure and reliable way.

2-5 e-municipality

It is an organization who uses IT to perform different services in the urban field, fast and secure. This organization acts exactly like the other municipalities and the only difference is that they use IT as a tool in performing better urban services. The following description is a total definition for an e-municipality: It is an organization that uses IT to perform services in the field of municipalities' duties fast, reliable and secure.

2-6 e-citizen

It is actually a new term which is going to be formed in consequence with developing world information society. This concept is very near to electronic life. An e-citizen is someone who is capable to use IT in his daily life and is able to use e-services of the e-city. An e-city has chosen itself a special life style, in this life style, entertainment, training, communication and individual transactions are done electronically. According to the surveys the following definition is for e-citizen: A person who is familiar with IT and is able to use e-services in an e-city.

2-7 Relations

Let's talk about the relations among the above items. One of the digital benefits for the citizens is that they are in the middle of concern for this reason the core philosophy of an e-government, e-city, e-municipality is performing suitable services to the citizens these connections and relations are shown in figure (2-1).

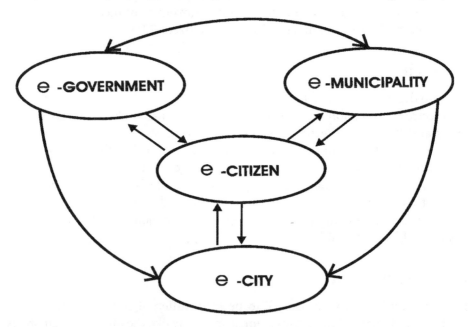

Figure (2-1): Connections and relations

2-8 Methodology

The methodology of the current project is based on studying the existing strategic models and interfering innovations and inventions related to the subject. This methodology has five basic components.

1-Concepts and literature of the subject
*e-government concepts
*e-city concepts
*e-city benefits
*e-city services
2-Adjustment scrutiny on the world situation
*e-government situation in the world
* Developed countries in the field of e-government
* Research works on e-cities in the world
3-Scrutiny and analysis of the existing situation
* Scrutiny on the accomplished steps
* Scrutiny on the IT situation of the city and the municipality of Mashed
*e-city from the manager's point of views
4-Codification of the proper situation of e-city of Mashed
* Codification of the vision of e-city of Mashed
* Codification of strategies and policies of e-city of Mashed
5-Identifying the strategic plans to reach the proper situations and goals
* Codification and implementing e-city of Mashed

The methodology is a centralized model that has focused on e-municipality and its implementation in the municipality of Mashed. In fact e-city, e-citizen and e-municipality have been studied based on the municipality and e-city's programs and the patterns are made out of these pivots programs and the ICT master plan. The model which is used is an adjusted, innovated model and is the result of studying the most successful e-cities in the world with considering the existing situation. Figure (2-2) is a description of the methodology.

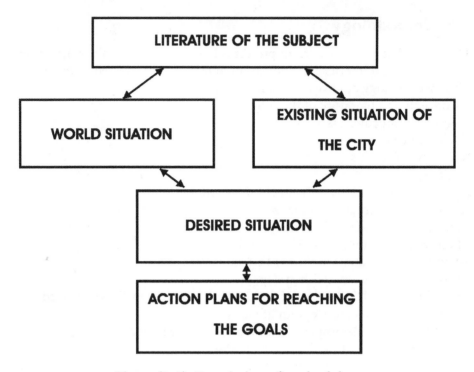

Figure (2-2): Description of methodology

2-9 e-city models

In this part we are going to study two different e-city models in the world. The first one belongs to Toronto and the second which was presented in the e-cities forum in 2002 in Thailand belong to Taipei.

2-9-1 e-city model for Toronto

From the point of view of Toronto e-city has the following strategic parts:
*e-government
*e-services
*Electronic commerce

e-government

An e-government describes the activities which are directly connected to the city council's operations. Its internal dimension includes upgrading management processes and decisions and its external dimension connects the citizens to the management levels.

e-services

This part consists of all urban web transactions and has internal and external dimensions. The external dimension offers reliable services to the citizens through internet and the internal dimension is centralized on the user's supporting services.

e-commerce

In Toronto's model EC consists of those projects, innovations and activities that support the business daily activities of the city and increase their operational productivity. This part has an internal dimension which is based on the integration priorities of the organization and an external dimension which refers to the new tools of commerce.

Infrastructure

The necessary IT infrastructures in making a city successful are:
*e-government
*e-services
*EC

These infrastructures are the basic cores for transferring information and technology and making the base of e-government, e-services and EC. The e-city prepares an operational and structural pattern for IT activities in the organization. e-city guarantees the IT investments and directs them towards the urban business units. The model of Toronto is shown in figure (2-3)

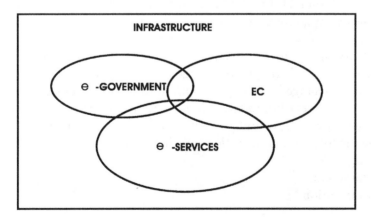

Figure (2-3): e-city model for Toronto

2-9-2 e-city model for Taipei

The e-city model for Taipei was performed in four sections as follows:
*e-life
*e-organization
*e-government
*e-infrastructure
   These four sections are shown in figure (2-4)

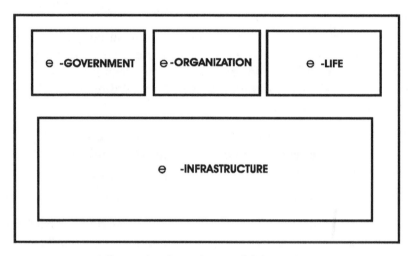

Figure (2-4): e-city model for Taipei

e-life

Through developing IT and the increasing effects of it on people's life another type of life style is going to be formed which is the result of the wide domain of the digital world on different aspects of human's life. Although the information age is still young but it has affected the whole human life. The theory of the world village is more highlighted through developing this age; people's life style has completely changed by using IT tools. In some countries like Singapore the theory of e-life is very hot today. In Singapore the government has focused on promoting proper culture and performing a desirable life style for the citizens. Generally the following four sections are known as the basic parts of an e-life:
* e-learning
* e-entertainment
* e-communication
* e-transaction

e-learning

Activating IT in the field of education and transferring educational concepts is called e-learning. This kind of training can be educated through the following items:
*Virtual schools
*Virtual universities
*e-learning while working
*e-learning and information dissemination for all the society classes in order to creating equal opportunities for the better life of all the citizens.

e-entertainment

Activating IT in delivering entertaining services can be as follows:
*Park information centers
*e-Tourist services
*Virtual museum and exhibitions
*Virtual libraries
*Virtual malls
*e-shops

e-communication

Examples of communication, sending and receiving messages through IT are as follows:
*e-mail
*e-chat
*CRM
*e-telephony
*ATM systems
*Info kiosk
*   ...

e-transactions

Today almost all the organizations and companies have their own web-sites and e-mails. ICT systems have made these companies' connections possible. IT can integrate them together and make them to have transaction with each other so, there will be few mistakes. Virtual teams can afford large scale projects. IT is facilitating the follow of globalization which is itself the result of digital world. Example of e-organization fields are as follows:
*EC
*e-services
*Human resource planning systems
*CRM

EC

Dealing through internet is called electronic commerce it consists enormous fields like business negotiations, marketing, advertising, e-payment, e-cards, e-services etc.

e-logistics

Today with the help of e-services, suppliers and customers are interacting with each other and are able to get their needs fast and easy. Monopolisem in this kind of market is almost meaningless. Different kinds of software are putting in use in this field like (SCM) which is an expert software in logistical operations.

Resource planning systems

These are some integrated softwares that cover all the processes and activities of the companies like ERP systems which are acting completely integrated now. These softwares are made up of individual modules and some of the most important of these are:
* Human resource management
* Accounting
* Product planning and management
* Payment system
* Documentation
* Warehouses

Applying these integrated systems will affect on cost reduction by dropping the traditional documentation which was paper consuming but it is paperless now and will reduce costs and time and will cease in clarifications of the tasks and easy follow of the processes, preparing suitable reports for management's logical deduction and increasing operational indexes of the company.

Customer relationship management

Today, most of the companies strategies are focused on being more customer oriented so, on this road CRM softwares are great help. By applying these systems companies can be aware of their customer's opinions fast, accurate and easy.

e-government

Applying internet and IT in governing the city and performing 24/7 services to the citizens is called e-government. In this new area of services the necessary information and services will be delivered based on the citizen's demands. e-government at least has four basic dimensions:

* G2G
* G2B
* G2E
* G2C

The new era in this field is e-governing which is not the physical body of the government but it is the process of managing the government and its structure.

Generally the following structure is defined for an e-government:

*e-government; inter relations that mean defining:
    1-Policies
    2-Implementing policies
    3-Performing public services

*e-management; internal organizational relations which consist of:
    1-Developing policies
    2-Organization's activities
    3-Knowledge management

*e-government; citizens, companies and governments which means:
    1-Democratic processes
    2-Open government
    3-Decision clarification

An e-government consists of the following items:

* Developing citizen oriented programs
* Developing citizen partnership
* Performing on-line information and services
* Measuring the web-sites and portals functions

e-management consists the followings:

* Strategic planning for performing on-line services
* Measuring and analyzing the on-line services costs
* Functional measuring
* Human resource management

e-government consists of the following:

*IT evaluations' effects on governmental processing
*e-federation
*Social challenges like digital gaps
*e-mortals, means corruption reduction and clarification scale up in functional operations

*e-democracy, means improving citizen's partnership, on-line voting, personal security and privacy
*Rules and regulations frameworks, means digital signature, copyright, tele-medicine rules and rights
*International challenges; virtual geographic boarders, information transactions
*Digital world effects and international standards

e-infrastructure

Creating an e-city without the proper infrastructure is actually impossible. The proper infrastructure in this field consists of the following four sections:

1-Rules and regulations
2-Human resources
3-Social situation and culture
4-ICT

1-Rules and regulations
Rules and regulations are necessary in order to characterizing and neutralizing IT cases in a digital world consist the following:
*EC rules
*e-payment rules
*e-banking rules
*Digital rules
*Copyright
*Telemedicine rules

2-Human resources
One of the important challenges in the field of IT is lack of experts. Unlike one's imaginations, human resource is the most important factor in digital world. In the third millennium in addition to land and energy another critic factor is human resource capabilities with the highest priority in the following areas:
* Human resource planning
* Human resource training
* Internet training for all
* Educated IT professionals

3-Social situation and culture
Improving IT in a society depends on the social and cultural situations. Without the proper infrastructure as mentioned before any kind of action plan is actually impossible, talking about the social and cultural situation consists the followings:
* Computer and internet permission factor
* IT applications

* IT accessibility among people
4-ICT infrastructure
ICT infrastructure is one of the most important bases in developing IT and consists of the followings:
* Increasing the rate of mobile phones
* Increasing the rate of internet hosts
* Increasing the rate of ISPs
* Increasing the rate of high speed optic fibers

2-10 Implementing an e-city

There are different opinions on implementing an e-city, each has its own views, and some of them are as follows:

2-10-1 Toronto e-city

According to the executive team in charge of implementing Toronto e-city, the project is completed through three stages:
1-Creating
2-Implementing
3-Stability
   The first step is creating and developing a strategic plan in order to implementing the e-city and defining necessary parts for making it executive. At this step SWOT process will be done and the primary design will be analyzed some of the objectives in this field are:
1-Citizen's accessibility to the city services 24/7
2-Optimizing urban resources
3-Selecting the best urban design for the city
4-Making the activities of an e-city meaningful
   In the second step the necessary infrastructure in implementing the designed e-city should be described, some of the objectives of this part is involving different working groups in the city to make the project into reality and finding solutions for the challenges which may occur, the results of this section are as follows:
1-Establishing hardware infrastructure in order to implementing the project
2-Developing security and copyright as an important part of the project
3-Cooperating with urban activities
4-Minimizing the overlapping activities
5-Minimizing the urban activities' time and cost
6-Optimizing the urban management

7-Integrating the business activities
8-Involving business companies in implementing the project and increasing productivity of the project
9-Optimizing the existing urban resources

In the third step the goal is performing a complete structured environment for IT and urban MIS. This is an endless step that by developing IT, it must be adopted.

The objectives of this step are:
1-Continuous evaluation
2-Upgrading the existing ITs
3-Accessing the strategic visions
4-Satisfying the business needs on-line

2-10-2 Taipei e-city

From the point of view of the founders and researchers of Taipei e-city, the project comes to reality in three stages:
1-Involving IT into urban activities
In this part the necessary IT tools and applications that can be implemented in the city will be identified and analyzed and put into the city activity process, the goal of this section is re-engineering the urban processes.
2-Electronic communication in urban activities
If we consider the first section as a part that has an internal view then it should be mentioned that the second part is external because it focuses on the ways of improving urban services for the citizens. The output of this stage is computer-ized integrated services. At this step the interconnection among activities are designed in a way that can be done and accessed electronically in this part the urban activity DFDs will be drowned and optimized.
3-Integrating activities
The third step focuses on performing an integrated system in order to facilitat-ing urban activities management with the help of IT in an electronically way.

2-11 e-city model for an Iranian city

Practical projects based on the world standards follow a designing cycle this cycle consists of four steps:
   1-Plan
   2-Do
   3-Check
   4-Act

1-Plan

The purpose of this step is planning the changes which will improve the existing situation. In this section primary surveys, analyzing the existing system, drawing different diagrams like Pareto help to identify the strength, weaknesses, threats and opportunities of the system which can be great help in performing suitable plan and finally improving the existing situation.

2-DO

The product of the previous section will be put in action in a small size in a small part of the system.

3-Check

After testing the prototype of the system, the plan will be put into feedback and will be checked in order to make sure of the accuracy of the prototype version of the system, the output of this section is planning some how guarantees the success of the execution of the project.

4-Act

The aim of this part is implementing the whole project and accessing the predicted objectives and benefits. The output of this section is planning the processes and their standards, taking the feedback of the system and performing necessary training for the processes the scheme of the design cycle is shown on figure (2-5):

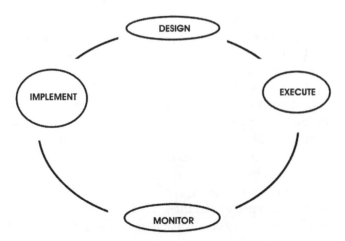

Figure (2-5): The scheme of design cycle

2-12 e-cities and e-municipalities in the globe, point of views

In this section first let's try to study the existing situation and future programs of the cities all around the world and continue with describing the visions and strategies of some of these sample e-cities this section will be continued through discussing the premium and services of these cities. SWOT will be described in this part and finally the first class e-cities and their executive companies will be discussed.

2-12-1 The existing situation and the future of e-cities in the world.

As mentioned before the municipalities and cities situations in relations with e-cities can be considered in four stages: creating, upgrading, interacting and integrity.

Some of the municipalities in developing countries are still in the first step means studying on the primary activities toward developing suitable master plan of creating an e-city and its culture. In the next step the municipalities try to develop their e-cities and e-municipalities; improving web-sites and their services, developing infrastructures, training the staffs are all in the action agenda of this part. Some municipalities are walking through this step. After passing this step web-sites are able to interact with each other which will cease in ease of e-relations of the citizens. In this section urban services are performed on web-sites and citizens can have on-line accessibility to urban services. Cities can be considered as a suitable background in putting e-government into reality. The successful e-cities in the world like Berlin and Boston are at the beginning of this part. Virtual organizations and Teleworking are some of the future features of e-cities. Following this program will cause traffic reduction and the staffs can afford their duties from distance as well as they work in their offices. Performing e-life style in the information age is another future feature of this program. Traditional life style will no longer be applicable in information age so, preparing a tailor made pattern for each society is another important program for the future of e-cities. In addition to all these attempts there has been some international activities done in the world like European union plan for integrating the European e-municipalities and putting them into interacting together. During this project an integrated system will be designed for the European municipalities in order to facilitate their activities. The European Union has invested more than 1.4 million Euros on this project.

2-13 e-cities as case studies

In this section we are going to study three cities: Boston, Indianapolis and Taipei and at the end of this part visions and missions of some other cities will also be pointed.

2-13-1 e-city of Boston

A. Introducing Boston
Boston is the capital of Masochists, a state in northern part of the U.S.A. There is a library in this city with almost 750000 titles. MIT which is one of the be loved universities in the world is located in this city. Boston is decreasing its development and has put its potential in gaining new technologies.
B. e-city of Boston
The portal of e-city of Boston has been very successful in transferring its contents to the citizens. The citizens have offered a wide accessibility to information, modules, surveying the reports to the citizens due to the city. On the first page of the city web page of the web-site based on being a simple citizen or a businessman one will be directed to the suitable part. Any users can access its necessary information. For example a tourist can access the city's information about the historical places etc. There are some areas in the city which are very popular for the people like the mayor's food court; this part is a virtual location for the reports about the restaurants and the quality of their foods and their credits. Another page is for e-payments. On different pages there is lots of information for the businessmen. When Boston came to this true that creating a web-site is vital for the city, with the corporate of Hitachi all necessary hardware were provided. Of course it should be mentioned that all the necessary infrastructure were prepared for the city and the architecture of the city in this field has been established accurately since the beginning. The city offers e-services for more than one million citizens daily with the cost of more than $ 200000 a day. The cost of creating the e-city of Boston at first consisted of 2 teams which have developed to 6 working teams now plus the software costs. Boston uses the latest web technologies. The mayor of Boston has had a deep concern about Boston's future since 1993. Mr. Menino the honorable mayor has decided to make the city a better place for life, work and joy. The mayor's priorities for the city are:
* Public security
* Education
* Urbanization
* Staff development

* Economic development

C. The effects of e-city on Boston itself

The web-site of the city has been completely successful. The site manager has claimed that most of the city characteristics have been more considered by people since the creation of the site. For example vehicle tax e-payment has had 300% increases between 1999 and 2000. In 2000 almost 3000 of the tickets were paid through internet monthly. There has been bureaucracy reduction, cost and time savings.

D. e-city of Boston characteristics

e-services which are performed through the city portal are as follows:

* On-line real states
* Tax and tariff information
* City events calendar
* Investment opportunities
* e-voting
* My Boston:
    My neighborhood
    My community
    My property
    My car
    My dog
    My voting status
*Who am I?
* Job offers
* City food court
* Found and lost
* My government
* Notification services
* Pay your parking tickets on-line
* Animal control
* GIS
* Real estate assessment
* Cemeteries
* Contact mayor's representatives
* Problem reports
* Business search

2-13-2 e-city of Indianapolis

A-Introducing the city
It is the capital of Indiana. It is the 12th largest cities in America with the population about 850000. It has occupied 403 square miles. The city is economically rich with 2.7 % unemployment rate. It has been said that Indianapolis is the crossroad of America.

B. City characteristics
The city site is very user friendly; citizens can access city facilities and services like the following through the city homepage:

*e-government
*Virtual societies
*Business
*Tourists and visitors
*Children

1-e-government
There is a link in this part to www.eGOV.org. In 1996 this part won the infrastructure government category award. The most important characteristics of this part are as follows:

*e-ticket payment
*Project reviews
*Mayor's attention centers
*e-tax payment

2-Virtual societies
This part produces very useful information on the following fields and offers them to the citizens:

* Real estate opportunities
* City official departments
* Public security information
* Environmental information
* GIS

3-Business
This section has been done by Civic Net, companies and businessmen and citizens can access the e-services and records on-line but by paying the costs, the features of this part are:

* Licenses information
* Purchasing
* RFQ

4-Tourists and visitors

There is a link to www.indy.org, in this part suitable information based on the tourists' tastes will be offered for example there is a link to the international airport.

5-Children

One of the unique characteristics of the city is its attention for the kids.

2-13-3 e-city of Taipei

A-Introducing Taipei

Taipei is located in northern part of Taiwan; Taipei is the political, economical, financial and cultural center of republic of china. It has thriving arts and academic scene and countless modern commercial buildings with its vibrant cultural and economic growth all these have made it into a modern international metropolis. Taipei has occupied 27177 hectares.

B-Goals and visions for cyber city building

* Increase the use of internet to decrease the traffic

Regardless how many and how fast roads are built to keep up with the growth in transportation demand Taipei will always run up against the limits of physical space, to solve this issue Taipei has focused on building public information network.

* Equal access to internet services for all

Democracy and economy are both premised on a few basic rights of the citizens. Just like the ability of citizens to own private properties and engage in commerce was a fundamental building block of the industrial age, in the information age every citizen must be entitled to the basic rights of access to modern information follows and networked services. Taipei believes that every citizen should have an equal opportunity to access the city public services on a fair and just basis.

* View internet services as public utilities

The internet is the most influential tools of the 21st century. In the future people will access internet to learn, consult, conduct business etc. It will be as easy and convenient as using today's telephones, television and gas.

* Create ubiquitous network of public services

In addition to its high educated workforce, one of the key components to Taipei's economic growth has been the ability of the public sector to cooperate with the private sector in creating an environment conductive to commerce

* To enhance Taipei's competitive advantage by bringing the internet to its people in an accessible manner.

By leveraging the internet Taipei has built itself into the most competitive world-class capital city in the region. The internet enables Taipei to enhance its position as an Asia-Pacific operations center for international corporations.
C-Program outline for Taipei
The following are the program outline for Taipei in order to creating a cyber city in the year of 2000. These overall goals are enhanced from the site of the city and studying them will clarify a total bright vision of this project.

Taipei's strategic overall goals

To achieve its vision and set of goals, Taipei has designed some accessible strategies as follows:
1-Service reform: "citizens as customers"
In building Taipei municipal government into a cyber city, Taipei first had to foster a paradigm shift that stressed customer service and aim to overcome limitations imposed by space, time and location to provide 24 hours a day, 7 days a week.
2-Process reform
To fully computerized operations, Taipei must re-engineer the design of the municipal government operational processes, so that civil servants become networked civil servants. This change will improve administration—processing efficiency while providing one-step full-service innovations to public.
3-Education reform
Taipei will establish cyber-universities and life-time learning centers as well as build diversified and universal channels for life-time learning.
4-Building an information infrastructure
Taipei is strengthening the development of the municipal government information infrastructure. Just as canals and railroad tracks were critical components of a city's well-being in the industrial age, the foundation of a city's success in the information age lies in its information infrastructure. To do the most effectively, Taipei is parenting with broadband networks of private enterprises. In the short run, these initiatives will connect Taipei's citizens to the internet at the lower cost then currently available. In long run, these efforts will lay the bedrock upon which future IT development in Taipei can build.

Taipei's broad strategies in implementing the cyber city

Taipei has designed the following broad strategies to achieve its vision and set of goals in the year 2000:

Strategy 1-Infrastructure foundations: build and deploy a high capacity information infrastructure in Taipei

Taipei is integrating the broadband networks of the private enterprises and building a high speed, high quality broadband service network in Taipei. In this way Taipei is able to connect every agency, school, community, hospital and home. It will enable Taipei to quickly move into a fully networked living environment. A city-wide information network will be built on the model of MAN (metropolitan area network). Additionally all city government agencies will be connected through an ADSL broadband network. Instituting an e-signature mechanism to issue citizen e-identification cards is under construction and implementation. Taipei is trying to set up an internet emergency response team. She also plans to establish a network maintenance and security management system within Taipei city government. Taipei will mobilize scholars and experts from all sectors to safeguard public internet security, and to protect public interests and rights.

Strategy 2: People: promote universal cyber-education

A 3-hour, on-line training course to residents of Taipei has been drawn to offer on the government's, schools', communities' and private sectors' computer classrooms and on-line activities and competitions in order to encourage citizens to acquire and sharpen their internet skills. Taipei will found public cyber-universities and public life-time learning centers to encourage the citizens to utilize the internet in educational setting. These efforts will improve the public's information skills. At the same time it will tap multimedia and distant learning technology to provide diversified learning and consulting channels. Information hardware has been, or it is being, installed in schools at all levels. To complement this hardware investment. Teachers are also encouraged to take on-line training classes to assist them in employing information education at all levels. In addition to setting up a computer lab at every school, it is expected that within 3 years every classroom in every high school, vocational schools, middle school and elementary school will have a computer. Internet education will become part of the curriculum for all subjects. This approach allows for the implementation of hands-on familiarity with information technology. As people grown up with the internet, they are quickly becoming the vanguards in the building of the cyber city. An e-library will be set up to allow the public to contact research directly through the network. The public will no longer need to travel to libraries to look up any information.

Strategy 3-Internal government re-engineering: informational government administration

In year 2000 almost 435 agencies and schools under the jurisdiction of Taipei municipal government have deployed EDI system. By outsourcing the building of information services Taipei tap the strength of the private sector in the information industry. Doing so, Taipei accelerates the building of cyber city government that easily and confidently provides various services to the public. A municipal government municipal data center has currently been created to facilitate the exchange of information among different government agencies. This part will offer information for decision makers as well. Taipei has occupied civil servants with computers so, PC has become an integral tool for the workplace. Its cost is less expensive when compare to personnel labor cost.

Strategy 4-Tapping information technology to improve service to the public

To improve the public services and services for the public, all agencies in municipal government were required to set up a web-site to provide on-line services. This effort was done in 1999 but every year there is a performance review of these sites. Paperless municipal services are increasingly becoming the norm. Taipei offers every one a free permanent e-mail address which will act as a linking bridge between citizens and the municipal government. Taipei will set up information kiosks in public places throughout the city. By year 2003 more than 800 units were installed around Taipei.

Strategy 5-Non-governmental public services

The plan of establishing 9 various public life networks has been initiated and is currently underway. It will be completed in 2007, on this network public safety, voluntary services, healthcare and medical services, community services, welfare assistance and other social services are available. Taipei plans to broaden the scope and content of the municipal characters. Within the legal limits, Taipei intends to make the information of the government data centers available to all the public and information industry on a subscription basis by linking the data to the public life network. Further to the discussion the summary of the strategies, plans and their related programs are in table (2-2):

Strategy	Plan item	Implementation plan
1-build an information Infrastructure implementing body	1-strengthening network building	1-promotion of wide frequency network building
	2-issuing citizens with Electronic ID Strengthening network security	1-issuing of citizen's ID 2-building of an information security mechanism 3-establishment of a network emergency response team
2-universalize network educational implementing body: bureau of education	1-plan and promote a life long learning network	1-learning net 2-open cyber university
	2-increase citizen's information level	1-free three hours of internet tuition for citizens
	3-actively promoting primary and middle school information network education	1-improve school information equipment 2-on-line training for teachers
	4-establishing an electronic library	1-establishing an electronic library
3-informational government administration work implementing body: Information center	1-building of an on-line city government	1-building of city government information net 2-promotion of internet in each government body 3-promotion of official work mail boxes for section office staff 4-establishing of a city government data bank

	2-strengthening of net-work civil servants	1-strengthening of staff information training so that each member of staff has the ability to go— online and use the PC to handle official work
	Reassessment of organization	Promotion of residency certificate and book free service
		Revision of information center organization
4-convenient service automation implementing body: research, develop-ment and evaluation commission	1-promotion of residency certificate and book-free service	1-promotion of residency certificate and book-free service 2-applications forms on-line
	2-single window service	1-promotion of one-stop document delivery, whole process single window service
	3-provision of 24 hour service	1-promotion of vari-ous bodies service going on-line 2-telephone/fax network information service
5-citizen's nine info net-works. Implementing body: information center and research, develop-ment and evaluation commission	1-free electronic mail-box	1-provision of lifelong elec-tronic mailbox to citizens
	2-promotion of social services network	1-safety net 2-charity net 3-community net 4-medinet 5-welfare and relief net 6-establishment of neigh-borhood and community web-sites

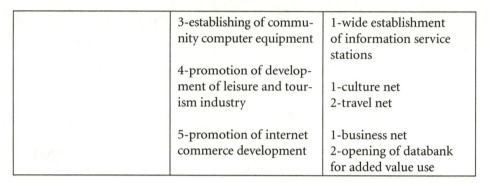

	3-establishing of community computer equipment	1-wide establishment of information service stations
	4-promotion of development of leisure and tourism industry	1-culture net 2-travel net
	5-promotion of internet commerce development	1-business net 2-opening of databank for added value use

Table (2-2): The summary of the strategies, plans and their related programs

Anticipated benefits

The summary of the anticipated benefits are:

1-Providing Taipei citizens with high speed and high quality wide frequency network services.

2-Providing Taipei citizens with diverse learning channels and an excellent life-long learning environment, to improve the quality of people's lives.

3-Universalization of information education and internet use, so that Taipei citizens become modern internet citizens.

4-Strengthening city government staff IT application capability to provide more convenient service to citizens.

5-Promotion of city government information flow, increasing administrative efficiency, so that Taipei becomes a highly effective international metropolis.

6-Allowing citizens at any time to easily go on-line and enjoy all the city government services

7-Satisfying the citizens "one stop document delivery" requirements, cutting down the number of applications people have to make to various bodies and reaching the target of reducing the volume of residency certificates and books.

8-Strengthening Taipei city's business competitiveness and create more business opportunities with commerce.

9-Making Taipei a place where it is easy to business, be educated, receive medical treatment, engage in leisure and live.

10-Promoting the overall development of Taipei and creating competitive advantage.

Recognized estimation indicators for evaluation the effectiveness of the city

Taipei has recognized the following estimation indicators to evaluating the effectiveness of the plan's implementation:

* Service re-engineering
* Process re-engineering
* Learning re-engineering
* Information infrastructure building

2-14 some e-municipalities samples

The following tables(2-3, 2-4, 2-5, 2-6, 2-7, 2-8) introduce some e-municipalities .

City	Virginia
Country	USA
Vision	Creating a life time society
Policies	Increasing physical, social, economical, educational life quality and qualified services for all
Strategies	Strategic thinking Increasing citizen's income Increasing useful activities Creating a positive view in people's mind Interaction and partnership Variety monitoring Proper decision making
e-services	Information for all Secure society On-line price information City council activities e-ticket On-line assessment Job information Job applications Schools and libraries Papers and magazines Contact media Safety points
City web-site	www.vbGov.com

Table (2-3): Virginia

City	Toronto
Country	Canada
Vision	Involving citizens in urban management Increasing political and managerial decision process New services for business men Increasing the rate of business in the city Supporting urban offices based on existing international standards
e-services	Urban transfer information Society events Health care Environmental Business licenses Urban tenders Tourists e-city council On-line job applications Urban rules and relations City events calendar On-line requests forms
City web-site	www.city.Tronto

Table (2-4): Toronto

City	Taipei
Country	Taiwan
Vision	Increasing internet in order to decreasing traffic Internet for all Ubiquitous life network
Policies	Increasing competition in Taipei to make it a world class city Replacing limited physical space with unlimited cyber space
e-services	Taipei GIS Taipei historical information Population information Climate information Urban transfer information Currency information Official work hour Emergency phone numbers

Related projects	e-Taiwan project Offering equal opportunity for software producers and suppliers Increasing industrial competitive and converting Taiwan into a world IT class island in Asia
City web-site	www.taipei.gov.tw

Table (2-5): Taipei

City	Indianapolis
Country	U.S.A
Vision	Excellent service to all parts of the city Facilitating ease of use of information
Policies	IT standards, IT guidelines and patterns re-engineering Reviewing IT policies Annual reviewing of budgets and IT projects Monitoring the services level Reviewing IT projects to facilitate citizen's affairs Supporting IT service providers Encouraging IT researches
e-services	On-line ticket payment On-line reporting service GIS On-line license issuing On-line purchasing e-entertainment Contact with mayor
City web-site	www.IndyGov.org

Table (2-6): Indianapolis

City	Arlington
Country	U.S.A
Vision	A world class city for life and entertainment
Policies	Involving citizen's partnership
e-services	On-line interactions GIS On-line ticket payment

	On-line tax accounting On-line city council Tourist on-line
City web-site	www.ci.Arlington.tx.us

Table (2-7): Arlington

City	Boston
Country	U.S.A
Vision	Useful content for the citizens
Policies	Educational qualification Continuous management Applied training Capacity improvement Management efficiency Upgrading lifestyle Parallelizing financial resources with city visions in the field of IT
e-services	Real estate City calendar e-voting My Boston Who am I Job advertisement City food court Lost and found My Gov Safety services Tax on-line Business places search Facilities search Cemeteries search Problem reports Business search City events Contact with mayor
City web-site	www.cityofBoston.gov

Table (2-8): Boston

2-15 e-cities visions

In the following chart some e-cities visions are listed:

no	city	country	vision
1	Boston	U.S.A	Useful content for the citizens
2	Virginia	U.S.A	Creating a life time society
3	Indianapolis	U.S.A	Excellent service to all parts of the city Facilitating ease of use of information
4	Taipei	TAIWAN	Increasing internet in order to decreasing traffic Internet for all Ubiquitous life network
5	Desmonies	U.S.A	Useful content for the citizens
6	Arlington	U.S.A	A world class city for life and entertainment
7	Toronto	CANADA	Involving citizens in urban management Increasing political and managerial decision process New services for business men Increasing the rate of business in the city Supporting urban offices based on existing international standards

Table (2-9): e-cities visions

2-16 Anticipated benefits of e-cities and e-municipalities

An e-city brings a new management infrastructure to the city and puts it into organizational change. There are a lot of anticipated benefits in the connection between the mayor and citizens and vice versa, and also between citizens, mayor and businessmen and vice versa. Some of these benefits are listed below:

1-Providing high speed and high quality internet services
2-Providing different training procedures
3-Improving life-style quality
4-Performing one-step services to the citizens

5-Amplifying business competition and creating business opportunities by applying electronic commerce
6-Better and easy organizational connection and interaction
7–24/7 on-line services
8-Involving citizens partnership
9-Traffic reduction through applying internet
10-Weather pollution reduction
11-Directing investment based on the needs
12-City problem solving through direct contact
13-Saving time and energy
14-Preventing more investing on the traditional city management procedures
15-Establishing necessary infrastructure for the development of the city
16-Office corruption reduction
17-MIS
18-Increasing people's awareness
19-Constant city income through an stable financial currency in the society
20-Cultural dissemination
21-Urban management and supervision

2-17 e-city services

Different surveys on e-cities all around the world has proved that most of the wide area e-cities services can be summarized in the following categories:
1-Related services with citizen's life
2-City's business services
3-Tourism and information dissemination services
    The first category consists of those services which are necessary for the citizen's better life. The seconds are those services which are useful for facilitating the business flow in the city and the third are those services which are useful for the tourists and visitors. These are not individual services; they are not only integrating each other but also complementing each other. In table (2-10) there is a list of e-cities services in the world. They are the results of surveying world class e-cities in developed countries like U.S.A, Canada, Germany, Japan etc, of course basically they are Americans cities and the reason is that there is a fine infrastructure in these states and there is a wide service domain than the others so, they are able to perform more wide vision toward the aspects of the accessible e-services in e-cities.

no	Service title	description
1	Voting forms	Sending and receiving voting forms
2	My city	City information
3	Who ma I?	Information about the neighborhood
4	Job advertisement	Looking for job through considering the related fields
5	City food court	Reviewing monthly reports on restaurant and their ranking
6	Found and lost	Information about lost and founds things
7	My Gov	Accessing government reports through password
8	Awareness services	City events based on the interests
9	Tax	On-line tax payment
10	Ticket payment	Ticket payment
11	Animal licenses	Animal licenses
12	Searching the facilities	Libraries, parks, resorts etc
13	Average citizens age	Sending citizens' profiles to the municipality annually
14	Cemeteries search	Cemeteries search
15	Contact with city council	Counseling with the city representatives
16	Problem reports	Awaking the mayor of the city problems
17	Contact with mayor	Direct contact with mayor
18	Ticket e-payment	On-line ticket payment
19	Real estate information	Preparing equal opportunity for the citizens
20	Urban organization information	Citizen's accessing to urban official information
21	Public security information	Citizen's awareness of the security procedures
22	Environmental information	Weather and climate information
23	GIS	Receiving proper information to accessing different parts of the city easily

no	Service title	description
24	On-line purchasing	Performing pricelists
25	TV programs schedules	TV programs schedules
26	Children	On-line entertainment for kids
27	Police on-line	Putting the accidents on the show
28	Court	Information about authorizes
29	Mails' information	Following the mailed packages information
30	City transferring	Time schedules for buses and metros and routes
31	On-line tax estimation tool	Estimating taxes based on the urban rules and regulations
32	e-reservation	Ticket reservation for concerts, cinemas etc
33	Schools	Schools information
34	Libraries	Libraries information
35	On-line publishing	e-magazines and journals
36	Real estate search	Citizens access to buildings lands etc
37	Project review	Putting the reports of the process of the projects on the web
38	RFPs	Accepting RFPs on the web
39 40	City trends City calendar	Putting the trends information on the web City events
41	Investment opportunities and resources	Performing existing potentials for investment
42	Business search	Integrating business databases
43	Business buildings search	Searching for the best business fields
44	On-line tourist	Performing tourists interests
45	GIS	Geographical information system
46	History of the city	Separated by title
47	Population	The city population, mortality and birth rate
48	Airlines schedules	Airlines information schedules

Table (2-10): List of e-cities services

Of course it is noticeable that not all the e-services are mentioned in the previous table. Some of those services are information dissemination services and some are electronic services. e-services needs the proper infrastructures and are in higher priorities of the city. In figure (2-6) and table (2-11) the frequency of the services in some e-cities are shown:

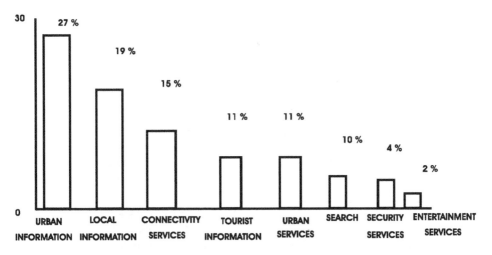

Figure (2-6): Frequency of urban services

VIRGINIA	INDIANAPOLIS	ARLINGTON	TAIPEI	TORONTO	BOSTON	DOSELDORF	ESHTOTGART	SERVICE
1	2	1	4	3	3	3	4	Habitance Environment Population Geographic
3	3	1	4	6	3	4	5	City calendar Trade History Rules Municipality organizations City council transportation

VIRGINIA	INDIANAPOLIS	ARLINGTON	TAIPEI	TORONTO	BOSTON	DOSELDORF	ESHTOTGART	SERVICE
1	1	1	1	1	1	2	2	Entertainment Exhibition TV programs Airlines
1	1	0	0	0	0	0	1	Games Museum Library
4	3	2	2	0	2	2	3	On-line journals Contact with mayor Contact with city council City chat room
1	0	1	0	2	4	1	3	Real estate search Job search Business opportunity Urban facility Historical places Urban trades restaurants
3	2	0	0	0	0	0	0	Police information Contact with police Firefighting departments

VIRGINIA	INDIANAPOLIS	ARLINGTON	TAIPEI	TORONTO	BOSTON	DOSELDORF	ESHTOTGART	SERVICE
1	0	2	0	1	0	4	3	Request forms for bids and trades Request forms for production Tax payment Ticket payment voting Request for identification card

Table (2-11): Frequency of the urban services in sample e-cities

2-18 e-cities in the world

As IT develops more cities are attracted to join the e-cities in the world. Most of these are formed in developed countries. It is noticeable that two essential methods are always involved in developing e-cities. The first development method is concerning development as preparing the proper infrastructure for IT, like internet city of Dubai. The second method is using IT applications for performing proper urban services. Mashed is basically using the second one of course sometimes both are putting in use.

Keeping our discussion for example Silicon Valley has used the first method and Taipei has chosen the second one.

2-19 Strengths and weaknesses of e-cities

Different types of e-cities have their own strengths and weaknesses, some of them are mentioned as follows:

Weaknesses

1-Increasing people's expectations
By improving urban services and updating citizen's life style it is obvious that people's expectations from the city grow up so, e-cities have heavier responsibilities against citizens so, most of the cities resources must be put into good use to satisfy these expectations this feature by itself can be named as a weakness point because satisfying all expectations is not an easy job.
2-Security
It is one of the issues which should be highly considered. A secure infrastructure is needed for preventing the private overpasses otherwise the city won't be reliable anymore.
3-City dependency to digital technology
One of the problems which can occur is the city dependency to IT this will cause the flow of the tasks into trouble if the city becomes addicted to IT.
4-Lack of IT professionals
It can be a serious problem after IT infrastructures, solving this problem needs a continuous planning and improving the knowledge of the mind workers.

Strengths

1-Job opportunity creation
Each new technology demands for a new field of specialization. This new field will cease to new job opportunities so, by creating an e-city there will be plenty of job opportunities and thousands of people will be put into their suitable jobs.
2-Proper infrastructure
It is a good background for the other new technologies and there will be a lot of cost savings for the future developments.
3-Globalization
Internet connection and upgrading IT level in the city and society will results in the growth of the society and will make the city a world class city.
4-Proper life style quality
One of the advantages of an e-city is preparing a qualified life style for the citizens and performing services based on the citizen's needs and requests which will result in increasing life style quality.
5-Fair distribution of urban services
Office functional tasks reduction, bureaucracy reduction, unlimited internet, self functional urban activities will finally result in fair distribution of urban services.

6-24/7 city.
24 hours accessibility 7 days a week is one of the e-city characteristics. Holidays, eves, and ... do not count as limitations in an e-city.

2-20 The basic challenges in e-cities all around the world

In the research process of an e-city and being benefited of its advantages are basic challenges which must be highly considered in order to defining suitable solutions, the most important key features in a successful e-government are:
* Investment
Creating and developing an e-city requires a large amount of capitals and investment in public sector. The money consuming parts are preparing ICT infrastructure updating computer systems, updating networks, wide training and so on.
* Software limitations
Internet is the most basic infrastructure in creating e-Gov and e-city in the world. There are billions of web sites over the internet, basically in English. There are still some problems with the IT services and local languages in some countries.
* Internet accessibility and digital gap
Based on 2004 statistics some about 900 millions use internet all around the world. 50 % of this population lives in America, Canada and Europe it is obvious that Asia and Africa's proportion is not comparable with them. Lots of people are still suffering from lack of internet accessibility. Without proper accessibility to the internet actually e-public services and e-urban services is practical meaningless. Reduction the digital gap guarantees it and is the most important initiative process in order to putting e-government into reality.
* Security and privacy
One of the basic worries in internet and cyber space is supporting people's security and privacy. People's personal and professional information are stored in urban data bases, by increasing the penetration percentage, these services will put the citizens in danger so, security and privacy protection policies are the most important challenges for the urban civil staffs.
* Training
From the aspect of city developments, training can be discussed in 2 dimensions: public information dissemination and preparing citizens for applying e-services and the second is training staffs for working in an e-city.
*Change management
Considering the different dimensions of e-government and its penetration percentage, change and mutation in people's urban life and governmental rules

and regulations, it is obvious that in order to having a more effective e-city these changes must be done through an effective management. Training, information dissemination in control planning of programs and providing the feedback of executive programs and analyzing them are some of the techniques and tools in change management.

* Social and cultural challenges

Different type of cultures, unlimited freedom, and accessibility to variety of information are the basic challenges in ICT fields through the world and especially the developing countries. These countries are much more sensitive in interacting through internet because of their social and cultural conditions. Based on the country and social conditions there has been a lot of success in security and control mechanism it is advised to consider them before creating an e-city.

2-21 World famous companies in the field of implementing e-cities

Creating, implementing and establishing an e-city needs an integrated cooperation between the governmental and non-governmental organizations. The planning and policy phase is usually done by the governmental departments and implementing an e-city project is usually done by non-governmental departments because they are more experienced. Some of the most famous companies in this field are Civic Net in America and E-Munis in Europe.

Chapter 3

MACRO PLANS

3-1 Macro plans for e-city and e-government in Iran

During the past few years there have been plans and programs to facilitate the creation of e-government in Iran but there weren't any macro plans in the field of e-cities of course some of the present projects can be used as a background in creating an e-city. In this section the most important steps in the field of e-government in Iran as the prototype society will be discussed and then the e-government indexes in Iran will be mentioned and at last but not at least Mashed and the municipality of Mashed will be discussed.

3-2 Research for e-government in Iran

Official council on its 93rd session held in 2003 approved the research plan for e-government on the following themes : accessing to accurate and up-to-date information in different economic, social and cultural sections through automating the activities, increasing the executive speed of the civil affairs, improving service providers with the maximum accuracy, increasing the quality of decisions in different levels, performing e-services, reducing the costs and increasing productivity by increasing efficiency and effectiveness in various sections and providing fast information distribution among executive departments all in coordinating with putting the e-government into reality.

1-Private activities automation

* Identifying, reviewing, and reengineering and mechanizing 10 characteristic processes in the executive offices which are in higher priority from the following point of views: Volume of activities, geographical widening, sample society, rate of e-communications and e-services.

* Establishing local information network and linking it to the global internet.

* Putting all necessary information for the citizens on the internet like the different processes, forms etc.
* Establishing a portal with the name of Mardom by the management and planning organization in order to facilitating information access.
2-Public activities automation
* Drawing up and approving formats, standards and characteristics of mechanized systems by the management and planning organization with the help of ministry of economic and finance and conveying them as official orders
* Providing and updating public softwares and choosing the optimized software among the existing softwares and introducing and advertising them to the executive offices
* Presenting required information for the management and planning organization like the labor laws, staffing, budgeting and credit allocation for the official organizations over the internet and information networks or even on disks or CDs.
3-Operating national identification numbers
4-IT training for the governmental staffs
5-Implementing and facilitating infrastructures
6-Providing legal infrastructures

3-3 TAKFA plan in Iran

The excellence council of information dissemination conveyed TAKFA in order to better and proper usage of IT capabilities which was approved by the Islamic cabinet on June 2003. This macro plan consists of vision, mission and goals and objectives related to IT development in Iran. In these master plan 7 strategic plans in the macro field of IT development in Iran has been seen. Each consist all executive projects and sub-projects that at the end point to the prescribed goals. In this section the overview of this master plan and its executive projects in the field of e-government has been discussed.

Vision:

* Powerful Iran in 21st century: knowledge base economic through ICT applications

Mission:

* Changing opportunities and national resources to wealth power and honor in the direction of national sustainable developments

Key strategies in providing ICT plans:

* Systematic development of ICT in national sustainable development
* Human resource development as the first priority in ICT strategic development plan
* Increasing synergy in the environment
* Providing infrastructures consists of: accessible network, rules and regulations, resources and facilities
*Involving private section as a key and strategic axis to move toward the ICT development

TAKFA goals:

* Upgrading the services efficiency by cost reduction and increasing public satisfaction
* Emerging and evolving citizen's partnership in the e-society
* Citizen's accessibility to the official information
* Country economic blooming with the help of digital economy
* Increasing job opportunities
* Creating new infrastructure in goals and services exports
* Decreasing digital illiteracy in a digital environment
* Fast and free accessibility to the ICT
* Increasing corporations and partnership between government and industry and public or private universities tuned with the task and the capital
* Increasing the knowledge of official managers about the role of ICT as a forwarder in all economic and social levels
* Performing the best ICT based processes
* Supporting the related private sector
* Increasing the growth rate of the small and the medium size enterprises in the field of ICT
* Advertising Islamic national culture in digital environment

Key domains in TAKFA

The basic sections of TAKFA are as follows:
* National master plan
* Developing proper infrastructure for human cultural and social resources
* Government administrative domain
* Developing commerce and economy
* Industry and occupation

TAKFA strategic plans

* Strategic plan for e-government
* Strategic plan for ICT applications in education and developing the digital skills of staffs
* Strategic plan for developing ICT in different ministries
* Strategic plan for ICT in social services
* Strategic plan for ICT in commerce
* Strategic plan for ICT in propagation of Persian culture and language over the internet
* Strategic plan for ICT in industry

TAKFA framework

The key domains in TAKFA are classified as follows:
* ICT macro plan
* ICT professional training
* Cultural dissemination of ICT
* Commerce with ICT tools
* National network infrastructure
* Rules and regulations in digital environment
* Occupation development in ICT field based on the growth of SMEs
* Industry development macro plan

e-Government strategies action plan

* Government virtual network
* Network management
* Rules and regulations
* Security
* Content

Budget planning automation

* Budgeting
* Agreement and settlement exchange
* Credit allocation
* Cost report
* Functional assessment
* Income and expenditure automation system

Governmental web-sites creation and people's accessibility to the governmental operational databases services

* Providing e-forms

* Providing databases related to each official department
* Providing MIS
* Facilitating the automation projects flow
* e-tender system

Providing the proposal of rules and regulation in digital government in the country

* e-crimes
* Authentication and digital signature
* Citizen's privacy support
* Conveying related standards
* Creating macro management e-city in domain issuing with extension ir
* e-courts
* Creating information highway infrastructures
* Establishing national portal
* Total integrated governmental network based on MIS

ICT macro plan

* Conveying national ICT macro plan, state ICT macro plan and ICT sectorization

3-4 National ICT macro plan

It is a master plan for ICT development in the whole country, its proposal was first published in 2003. The mission is coordinating all executive programs in the field of ICT in the country. There are many projects in these master plan especially in 3 fields namely: post, telecommunication and IT.

Vision

Digital gap reduction and moving tuned with the world strategies
* Increasing accessibility quantity
* Increasing accessibility quality
* Human resource training
* Cultural promotion for e-searching
* Dropping the governmental monopoly
* Updating the rules and regulations
* Defining standards for ICT indexes
* Integrated automation promotion
* Reforming the communication structures
* Attracting the national and international financial partnership

Programs and projects

1-Communication services updating
* Developing plan for fixed telephone
* Developing plan for cell phone
* Developing plan for network infrastructure
2-Post development program
* Developing plan for casual post
* Developing plan for financial post
* Developing plan for e-post
* Developing plan for national and international post
3-ICT application programs
* Data network development plan
* e-government development plan
* e-commerce development plan
* e-learning development plan
* Health care development plan
* ICT industry development plan
* Technology parks developing plan
* National language developing plan
* ICT culture promotion developing plan
* ICT export developing plan

Detailed programs for the plans related to e-government

* Providing e-government macro plan
* Providing e-government legal rules and regulation's plan
* LAN creation among state offices
* Improving and up-grading the basic hardware and software official offices
* Web-site designing for state offices
* Creating suitable organizational infrastructure in management and planning organization for coordinating the plans
* Increasing people's awareness of e-government
* Public and particular software development in the staffs' offices
* Implementing state databases
* Information interaction among state sectors
* Information interaction among private and public sectors
* Integrating public systems
* Executing especial integrated transactions through state departments

3-5 e-government indexes in Iran

In the table (3-1) some of the indexes are listed. These are based on the UN indexes in this field. In the named table not only Iran's indexes but the world average indexes are mentioned. It is obvious that Iran is almost under the average of the world. The weakest part is related to infrastructures. In order to putting Iranian government into the need of proper infrastructure the first priority is improving the IT infrastructure in the country.

Index	Country IRAN	World's ave.
Computer per 1000	5.88	10.17
Hosts per 1000	0.27	215.39
Internet access per 100	0.8	11.25
Tel. per 100	14.9	21.44
Cell phone per 100	1.51	15.3
Television per 1000	157	288.49
HR development index	0.714	0.731
Information access index	0.167	0.646
Urban population	61.6	61.9
e-government index	1.31	1.62

Table (3-1): UN indexes

3-6 The city of mashed

Cause of causes in a city creation and development are as follows: religion, security, economy, politic and administrations. A city is set forth as human, geographic, economic and social phenomenon which is born in especial condition and continuous to live and grow and change. These factors were also the cause of causes in creation of Mashed.

Mashed is the capital of Khorassan-e-Razavi. It is located in the northeast of Iran. The population of mashed is about 2.5 millions. There are more than 13 million tourists and pilgrims in mashed each year. Mashed is the second city in Iran. Tourist industry, existence heavy and semi heavy industries, agricultural products are the main revenues of the city. The city is rich and among the Iranians statmen Mashed has an especial situation for industrial and commercial investments. International airport, railway, proper banking network, proper communication infrastructure and many other factors has gifted the city a good situation in the country. All the above factors have made the city as one of the four pilot cities in the field of IT in the country's macro plans. Right now after Tehran, Mashed has the most capacity in accessibility to the public networks.

3-7 The municipality of mashed

In 1924 the municipality of mashed was established and called Cleansing and Light, during years it grew and in 1952 its name changed to municipality of Mashed and moved to the existing building. There has been 53 mayors in Mashed since then, 10 of them started their job as mayor after the revolution. Right now there are 6 deputyships, 12 zones, 14 organizations and about 84000 employees.

3-8 The history of internet in mashed

For the first time in 1993 Ferdowsi university of mashed established and started up the internet through the dial up connection 8 hours a day. The first and the only network node in Iran on that time was Iran's physic center. After a while information and stochastic center of Ferdowsi university of Mashed decided to make its own independent network and put it over the internet finally with team working of the mentioned centers a complete independent network was installed in that university. Related to this matter the information and stochastic center of Ferdowsi university of Mashed requested an IP address just for that network from the network manager which was in England on that time. Since then the network of the university of Mashed has been identified as a node with high credit and IP in class C.

In 1997 for the first time Khorasan data center provided the internet connection through X25 protocol. In 1999 Ferdowsi university of Mashed requested for internet through TCP/IP protocol. In 2002 the band width was 2 megabyte. Now there are 155 megabyte of optic fiber and 16 megabyte of microwave.

Since 2004 all the cities with the population above 5000 are connected to the internet through the width band of 2meg. Right now there are some about 75 active ISP companies in Khorasan.

3-9 The position of mashed in developing IT in the country

Mashed has been offered a key position in developing IT in the country and is one of the four pilots in the country. Here is a brief description of national development maps about the optic fiber network and the basic data centers in Mashed and Isfahan.

3-9-1 Various types of internet accessibility

There are three different categories:
* Internet accessibility through dial up connection
* Internet accessibility through E1
* Internet accessibility through leased lines

3-9-2 ICT policy making council in mashed

* IT strategic council
* IT strategies steering committee in municipality of Mashed

3-10 The strengths and weaknesses of Mashed e-city

A-Strengths
* Mashed as the second city in Iran
* Mashed as the capital of Khorasan
* Mashed as one of the four IT development pilots
* More than 13 millions tourists and pilgrims a year
* Proper economy and investment opportunities
* Attracting special attention of the public and private sectors
* Young population
* Low labor costs
* Having good profiles in executing different projects
* International airport
* High qualified universities
* Good ICT infrastructure
* Mashed as a good pilot for e-services promotion
* Accessibility to the local and national or international information
* Low service costs
* Low connection costs
* Large number of donators

B-Weaknesses
* Low computer penetration coefficient
* Low computer users' coefficient
* Low phone and cell phone coefficient
* Lack of internet hosts
* Lack of investments in IT section
* Bad quality of internet services
* Lack of rules and legal policies about security and privacy
* People's worries about security and privacy
* Lack of local professional staffs
* Lack of public digital literacy
* Lack of e-cards and payments
* Internet hackers
* Digital gap
* High prices of internet services
* Low speed
* Low efficiency of staffs
* Lack of software and hardware production
* Not proper resources allocation in developing IT
* Lack of organizations with dynamic websites
* Low volume of governmental services on the internet
* Lack of credit cards
* Lack of a complete e-banking services
* Lack of public culture on e-applications
* Lack of e-medical counselors
* High prices of computers
* Lack of IT directors
* Lack of proper information staffs

Chapter 4

MODELS

4-1 Suggested model

Considering the e-cities models and through using DEMING cycle the following model is suggested for e-city of Mashed:

1-Creating e-city
2-Executing
3-Monitoring and controlling
4-Implementing

The phenomenons of each above part are as follows:

1-Creating e-city
* Identifying the visions, strategies and urban policies in implementing an e-city
* Defining the applicable projects for the city
* Defining the necessary strategic projects
* Staff's training
* Information dissemination

2-Executing
* Processes and structures reviewing and probably re-engineering
* Involving IT in urban processes
* Defining urban activities electronically
* Executing strategic projects
* Citizen's training
* Performing some of the municipalities services electronically as a prototype and sample
* Monitoring and controlling
* Information management
* Change management
* System analysis and design

* Comparing the ex and the new systems
3-Implementing
* Integrating urban activities
* Conveying necessary standards in e-city field
* Creating the e-city web-site
* Establishing proper infrastructure for e-services
* Accessibility to all urban service and information through internet
* Regular reviewing of policies and programs and updating them

4-2 e-city functional assessment indexes

Based on the conceptual model in figure (2-4) an e-city has 4 basic sections:
*e-life
*e-organization
*e-government
*e-infrastructure
Considering the mentioned model the proper indexes for assessing e-life, e-infrastructure, e-organization and e-government are defined in table (4-1).

field	description	index
Internet connection	Computer and internet penetration	* Cell phone rate * Internet connection rate * Band width rate * e-learning * Schools band width * Housewives' internet accessibility to internet * Public network equipment accessibility

field	description	index
Social and cultural conditions	Education	Illiteracy rate Average of public training Political freedom rate Quality of public and private schools

Human resource	Mind-workers	Ratio of IT professional to the total employees Ratio of engineers to the total employees Ratio of organization satisfaction from its IT professionals Ratio of IT training to the total employees
Rules and regulations	Reliability of on-line processing and the existing information on the network	Supporting e-privacy Preventing e-crimes
ICT infrastructure	Accessibility to the communication systems	Potential in developing telephone services Telephone per 1000 persons Cell phone per 1000 persons Web hosts per 1000 person Cost and quality of telecommunication services

field	description	index
e-services support	Portals, host, ASP, ICP support	Professional information dissemination support Software products knowledge Comparability in market
Internet connection	Network connection price list	Network equipment ownership price Organizations connection to internet price Fast accessibility to organizations Web-site creation price Intranet creation price ICT equipment investment Ratio of ICT professional to the total organization's staffs Investment on ICT training
Learning EC	EC applications programs	B2B Organization's internet programs Investment on internet Online marketing

field	description	index
Internet connecting	e-government services and management	Efficiency of application programs Online police services e-government web-site creation Wide accessibility to state organizations Internet connectivity price for the government departments Network interaction prices for governments
e-leadership	Government policy in order to up grading e-society and coop-eration between public and private sectors	Governmental policy priority on ICT Investment by ICT support companies Encouraging organizations on investing on ICT Especial ICT trainings

Table (4-1): Different indexes in different fields of suggested model

4-3 Visions, missions, strategies and policies in e-city of Mashed

The most important part in master plan for creating (building) e-city of Mashed based on the municipality is conveying the vision, strategies and defining the ICT policies.

In this part first there will be definitions about the vision, followed by about strategies, policies and plans.

4-4 Definitions

In this part first there will be definitions of vision and then strategies, policies and plans.

4-4-1 Vision

Vision is a landscape which is not only comprehensive but clear and simple, it is a slogan which can direct and coordinate the motivations toward the goals of the organization vision causes motivation in the working environment and can be a proper functional index on organization success. Vision is from the type of quality and as the idol quality is not 100% accessible, vision is so. But it is probable to become as close as possible. There is a difference between goal, vision and strategic objectives. Vision is the idol situation of the organization. Having a vision even in technology development has helped the developed and developing countries to face a faster economic growth and success. A country like India with proper vision has made it to one of the IT powers in the world. Vision is a motivate factor to move towards the goals. Defining a vision in an organization will make all the staffs to be directed toward the common objectives and the final goal of the organization. Through this way the existing resources will be used more effectively. All dimensions of an organization must be covered by its vision and ceased to the blooming of that organization.

Some of the characteristics of the vision for developing e-city of Mashed are:

1-It clears the direction of the city path toward success by applying IT tools

2-All the urban activities are directed toward the objectives and fast qualified development are going to happen both theorical and practical in the official service and commercial fields

3-It authorizes the urban set of activities in the field of IT and makes citizens to feel proud of them

4-It motivates the feeling of cooperation and coordination among all urban organizations

5-It prevents critics and the corruption among organizations which will cease to cost reduction and tasks overlapping

6-Vision in municipalities will cease to correct and optimize decisions

7-Observing the successful image of the city will encourage the citizens' partnership in urban activities.

4-4-2 Strategies

Rossel Ackoff mentioned that each strategy must have the following characteristics:

1-must be far from details

2-must be totally organizational

3-must look far from execution

The point that should be mentioned is that any strategies without the above characteristics is priceless and must be ignored. Strategy is a float concept so the more macro the application of the strategy concept, the more efficient it will be. The other characteristic of strategy is that, it is totally procedural so, considering the above information in master plan of Mashed the strategy is defined as follows:

The decision macro step regulation for the whole organization related to the vision is called strategy, Of course it shouldn't be forgotten that basically strategy is a tool to move the existing situation toward the proper situation. As mentioned before the proper situation is the nearest one to the vision. Actually strategies are formed in 2 ways:

1-Bottom-up
2-Top-down

4-4-3 Policies

Policies are programs which hold decisions; they will be used as guidelines, frameworks or ideas in decision making process. Of course most of the time policies do not have a paper forms. Sometimes they are just made by the functional managers. Policies actually define the limitations of decisions and bring some indexes for surveying the amount of aids in order to reaching the goals. Policies are necessary for all the organizations levels. Let's describe the meaning of policy first," The set of all decision regulations in a single step is called policy."

Comparing with strategy, we see that policies are not as wide as strategies; in fact policies are the framework for strategies in execution and are the tools for directing them towards the goals.

4-4-4 Plans

Plans are set of objectives, policies and guide lines. Plans are usually supported by financial credits and budgets. Sometimes execution of a program needs the execution of some other sub-plans at the same time. The plans are scheduled and their priorities are mentioned.

4-5 Vision, strategy, policy and plan creating cycle

Vision, strategy, policy and plan creating cycle is shown in figure (4-1):

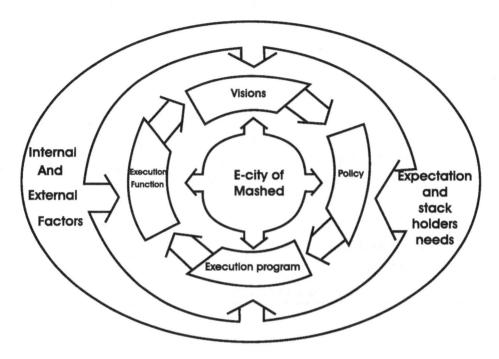

Figure (4-1): Vision, strategy, policy and plan creating cycle

4-6 Different IT aspects

A strategic plan will describe the position of all IT indexes and their affects on each other in the society. It also helps the organization in meeting its goals. Different IT aspects have been shown in figure (4-2):

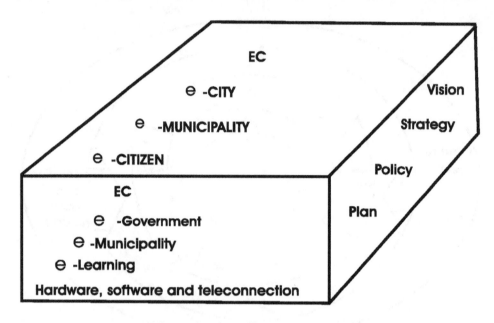

Figure (4-2): Different IT aspects

4-7 Visions, strategies and policies in e-city of mashed

In order to conveying the proper vision for e-city, e-municipality and e-citizens in the current project the following subjects have been surveyed:
* e-government vision in different countries
* e-city visions in different cities in the world
* Suggested vision for Mashed municipality
* The results of interviewing the civil staffs of the Mashed municipality
* S.W.O.T

    Of course it should be mentioned that TAKFA has drawn the e-government vision in Iran but based on the studies on other countries and the current situation of Iran, Two other visions are suggested for e-government in Iran.
A. e-government vision
* Knowledge base economy (TAKFA)
* Creating an information society
* Qualified life through innovation and rival
B. e-city vision
* Performing proper services 24/7 to the citizens and tourists
* Creating a world class city for life, work and entertainment
* Creating a dynamic economic environment

* Traffic reduction
* Process clearness
C. Municipality of mashed's vision
* Being customer oriented in urban management
* Accessing to the municipality services 24/7
* Fast, not expensive and up to date services
* Stable income currency for the municipality
* Clearance of processes
D. e-citizen vision
* A world class citizen for the world information society

e-city of Mashed strategies:

The following strategies are seen in the master plan of implementing the e-city of Mashed based on municipality
* Proper infrastructure with high capacity creating in municipality
* Intelligence monitoring related to urban services in the municipality
* Total training for the citizens
* Integrating the information and functional systems in the municipality
* Stable income currency making for the municipality
* Reviewing and improving the current necessary and effective processes in e-city
* Up-grating the service quality and staffs training
* Creating and implementing urban data bases

e-city of Mashed policies

In order to better decisions and decision making and parallel with the e-city visions the following policies are defined:
* Consuming the financial recourses in the same way to get the visions
* Preventing the parallel execution of the same tasks and convergencing the tasks and plans toward the vision
* Supporting the processes created for e-city
* Encouraging polices in order to developing IT in e-city
* Encouraging team working and partnership in municipality and e-city of Mashed.

4-8 Master plan for implementing e-city of Mashed based on the municipality

In order to convey the master plan for implementing e-city of Mashed based on the municipality, first the development model for the e-city is performed which is a dynamic model, structures in this model are periodically updated and injected to the different sections through a cycle form structure.

Developments are the results of developing technologies applying new tools always face new changes in the previous disciplines; it is noticeable that this model supports them, too. Following the above articles the suggested systems and plans for e-city of Mashed will be discussed. Based on the professionals and the researches done on the e-city phases in the world and the suggested phases by the involving companies and also based on the previous experiences of the pioneer cities on this matter, the following different phases are suggested for e-city of mashed of course it should be mentioned that the plans which are related to the hardware and infrastructures are not considered because of the existing situation of the municipality.

4-9 Suggested phases for the master plan of implementing e-city of mashed

Phase 1-Setting the stage for implementing (building) the e-city of Mashed
The goal is preparing a total framework for the project executions and the necessary trainings. In order to put this framework to true the following tasks must be done:
1-Approving the e-city laws
2-Performing e-facilities and web designing for the public and the private sectors and organizations in the city
3-Creating proper infrastructure in ministry of interior, the management and the planning organization
4-Increasing the public awareness towards IT and its capabilities
5-Training the IT professionals
6-Establishing the intranet among cities
7-Preparing the e-city documents
Phase 2-Practical planning
The goal of this phase is interchanging the traditional ways with the new IT ways
1-e-services for the citizens
2-Producing, distributing and applying the digital information in public and private organizations
3-Public training for citizens
4-Creating and establishing software systems for urban units
5-Reforming the urban management system based on e-city

Phase 3-Implementing

The goal in this phase is preparing the necessary standards and applying them in the whole system after testing by:

1-Creating information interaction among public and private sectors and Organizations

2-Creating information interaction among citizens and public and private sectors and organizations

3-Creating and developing the interactions trainings

4-Conveying the necessary standards for e-city

Phase 4-Integrating

The goal in this phase is the communication of all organizations, state officials and companies electronically after executing and stabling this part the continuous improvement will be put on top and phases starts to repeat from the beginning to the end again.

1-Creating public integrating system

2-Electronic transactions

3-Creating virtual, commercial, educational and health care organizations

4-Information transaction in the whole country

5-Information transaction with information society

6-Continues reviewing of policies and e-city programs

7-e-city system continuous improvement

4-10 Suggested phases cycle

The summary of the suggested phases is shown in figure (4-3):

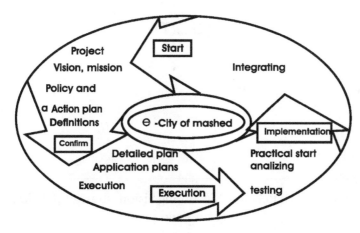

Figure (4-3): Suggested phases cycle

4-11 Necessary telecommunication infrastructures in Mashed

Mashed is one of the 4 pilots in Iran. There is almost no serious problem about telecommunication infrastructures in Mashed. In fact not only there is no problem but also the band width can be widened whenever necessary. It is noticeable that there are still a lot of vacancies on the current band.

4-12 e-city of Mashed plans and programs

All the suggested plans and programs are moving toward meeting the strategies and finally the visions of the city. The relationship among them is shown in the figure (4-4):

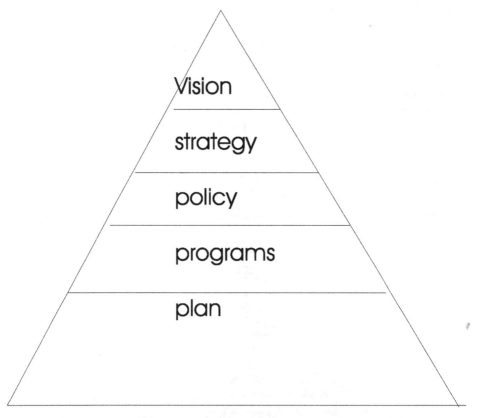

Figure (4-4): Relationship among vision, strategy, policies, programs and plans

Continuation of this part, the plans and programs in e-city of Mashed will be discussed, of course it is noticeable that in the process of suggesting plans the following priorities has been considered:
* High level management, professional urban staffs
* National ICT documents
* e-city of Mashed visions
* e-city of Mashed strategies
* e-city of Mashed policy
* Citizen's needs

Master plan

The following plans have been seen in the master plan for implementing e-city of mashed based on the municipality and its services:
1. Infrastructure development plan
2. Hardware development plan
3. Training and education plan
4. Paths and standards improvement plan
5. Encouraging financial plans
6. Information dissemination development plan
7. System development program
Each of the above programs consists of some sub-plans which will be discussed later.
A. Infrastructure development plan
Proper infrastructure is one of the basic necessary steps in developing an e-city. Infrastructure development plan in this master plan has been divided into three categories:
1. Urban infrastructure
This category consists of the telecommunication infrastructures in e-city of Mashed. Legal guardian for this part is ITC (Information and Telecommunication Company).
2. Infrastructure among organizations
This category is responsible for the communication among public and private sectors in Mashed. Through the suggestion of related organization and with the cooperation of ITC the necessary infrastructure will be conveyed.
3. Infrastructure base in the organizations
This means establishing the organizations LAN and releasing it on the internet, each organization itself is responsible for that.
B. Hardware development program
Some of the most important equipments in this part are as follows:
* Network hardware
* Data center hardware

* Users hardware
* Necessary hardware for accessing
* CPE tools
* Servers
* LAN tools
* Switching and multiplexing
* Hardware necessary for network management (NOC)
* Operational system support hardware (OSS)
* Testing and manipulating hardware
C. Training program
The best training programs in the field of e-city are as follows:
* Preparing the professional staffs as technical supports
* Increasing public cultures about e-city
* Public education
* Managers awareness of e-city

Point:

There has been considered a 6 character code for each suggested plan, the first one is D, the second one is for the domain's number(1-7), the next 2 characters are for the sub-domains(systems) and the last 2 characters shows the plans number. As mentioned D is for domain and the second one is for the domain's No. (1-7).
1-Infrastructure
2-Hardware
3-Training
4-Rules and regulations
5-Financial developments
6-System development
7-Information dissemination
For example D70304 means the 4th plan from the 3rd sub-domain related to the 7th domain. So, as shown in table (4-2) it is the 3rd sub-domain from the information dissemination domain which can be urban dissemination and of course its fourth plan which can be online commercial information. Or in short:
Information dissemination > urban information dissemination > online commercial information

Domain & domain's NO.		Sub-domain NO.		Plan's NO.	
D	7	0	3	0	4

Table (4-2)

D. Organization's program, rules and regulations
Because of the obvious differences between an e-city and a city, reengineering of rules and regulations are necessary. During the process of improving the current infrastructure a new organization for establishing and managing the e-city will be appeared. The suggested plans for that field are shown in table (4-3):

#	Domain's name: organization's program rules and regulations	Domain's code
	Plan's name	Plan's code
1	ICT strategic councils in e-city of MASHED	D40100
2	IT organization of MASHED	D40200
3	Providing definitions for key processes in the city	D40300
4	re-engineering and reviewing the urban processes	D40400

Table (4-3): Suggested plans in the field of organization's programs, rules and regulations

E. Financial developments (absorbing and developing financial resources)
Financial resources are listed in table(4-4):

#	Domain's name: financial resources	Domain's code: D5
	Plan's name	Plan's code
1	Absorbing financial resources from TAKFA	D50100
2	Absorbing financial resources from states budgets	D50200
3	Local credits for the e-city projects	D50300
4	Donator's support	D50400
5	International bank support	D50500
6	Private sector investment	D50600
7	Organization's credits	D50700
8	Foreign investment	D50800
9	NGO's support	D50900
10	Interior ministry support	D51000
11	Partnership support	D51200
12	Applying advertisement for increasing the city's income	D51300
13	Encouraging people for consecration	

Table (4-4): Financial developments

F. Systems development

The basic elements in an e-city are its systems, implementing and developing systems can be used as a good background for better e-services. The suggested systems in this project are listed in the table (4-5):

Program code	program	system	Sub-system	code
D6	System field	Integrated office system (D601)	Financial	D60101
			Personnel	D60102
			Call out	D60103
			Wage	D60104
			Facility	D60105
			Paperless	D60106
			Security	D60107
			Insurance	D60108
			Selection	D60109
			Properties	D60110
			Warehouse	D60111
			Budget	D60112
		Integrated e-services system(D602)	Blockade	D60201
			Machinery system	D60202
			Recycle system	D60203
			Cemetery system	D60204
			Fire fighting	D60205
			Greengrocers	D60206
			Green space	D60207
		EC-system (D603)	Auction	D60301
			Sales	D60302
			Purchase	D60303
			Trends	D60304
			Bid	D60305

		Urbanization inte-grated system (604)	Fraternity	D60401
			Revenue	D60402
			renovation	D60403
			Supervisor engineer	D60404
			Execution of orders	D60405
			Commissions	D60406
			Urban light train	D60500
			Tax accounting	D60600
			Ticket payment	D60700
			Traffic	D60800
			Transmission	D60900
			Taxi	D61000
			Bus	D61100
			Vehicle tariff	D61200
			Archive	D61300
			Project control	D61400
			Training	D61500
			Real estate	D61600
			Integrated library	D61800
			MIS	D61900
			Contractors	D62000
			Inter organi-zational com-munications	D62100
			GIS	D62200

Table (4-5): Suggested systems

Detailed definitions of the mentioned systems are mentioned in table (4-6):

System's name	Office automation system
Code	D601
Description	This system is consist of : accounting, personnel, call out, payment, facilities, paperless, security, insurance, assessment, warehouse and budget which will mechanize all the organization's internal activities
Characteristics	Work follow Office management Ease of processes Dynamic reporting system Form designing Work follow definition Security levels definition Web-based system
Users	All the municipality zones and departments and official organizations
System's name	Urban services
Code	D602
Description	The sub systems : blockade, machinery, recycle, cemetery, firefighting, parks and green spaces and GIS
Characteristics	Dynamic reporting Form designing Security levels definitions
Users	Municipality and its deputies and departments
System's name	Electronic commerce
Code	D603
Description	The sub systems are: sale, trade, bid, auction
Characteristics	Public friendly
Users	People, official organizations, municipality departments, trades
System's name	Urbanization
Code	D604
Description	The sub systems are: revenue, renovation, estate, supervisor engineers, orders execution and GIS

Characteristics	Dynamic reporting Form designing Work follow definition Security level definition Parametric ticket accounting
Users	Municipalities as the main users and trades and citizens as peripheral users
System's name	Light train
Code	D60500
Description	Controlling and monitoring the light trains in order to perform better services
System's name	Taxation
Code	D60600
Description	Recording the assessment information of the citizens, accounting the taxes amount, connection to the office integrated system, defining the level of accessibility to the system
Users	System users
System's name	Ticket payment
Code	D60700
Description	Accepting the tickets from info kiosks
Users	The public
System's name	Traffic control
Code	D60800
Description	Traffic management, travelers information, public transportation, critic management, security
Users	The organization of traffic control
System's name	Public transportation
Code	D60900
Description	Recording the arrival and departure information of the buses
Users	The public transportation organization
System's name	Urban transportation
Code	D61100

Description	Recording the urban buses to the parking and garages, controlling the buses in their paths, recording the buses identifications, complaints controlling and GPS
Users	The urban transportation organization and citizens
System's name	Vehicle taxation and tariff system
Code	D61200
Description	Recording the vehicle information and issuing tax tickets etc
Users	Different zones of the municipality
System's name	Archive and documentation
Code	D61300
Description	Defining the accessibility level to the documents, creating databases of documents, searching system
Users	Different zones of the municipality and the official organizations
System's name	Project management
Code	D61400
Description	Recording the project management information and resources, controlling the resources, project improvement, preparing the managerial reports for decision making, contacting to contractors
Users	Municipality departments
System's name	Training and education
Description	Recording the trainers and the trainees information and the courses
Users	Municipality departments and companies with more than 30 personnel
System's name	Estate system
Code	D61600
Description	Creating estate database
Users	Citizens and the municipality zones
System's name	Streets appellation
Code	D61700

Description	Preparing the streets identifications
Users	The municipality public affairs and zones
System's name	Integrated library
Code	D61800
Description	Recording all libraries information, connecting them, searching and membership
Users	citizens
System's name	MIS
Code	D61900
Description	Preparing necessary statistics reports for management and databases, assessing them and defining the accessibility levels
Users	Municipalities and their departments
System's name	Contractor's system
Code	D62000
Description	Contractors affairs, recording their information, contacting to the project control system
Users	Municipalities zones and related organizations
System's name	Organizational interactions
Code	D62100
Description	A connection bridge among the different organizations of the city and their interactions
Users	Municipalities, companies and official organizations
System's name	GIS
Code	D62200
Description	Accessibility to the maps and geographic information, creating maps databases, recording the geographical information and locations, connectivity to urbanization system, accessibility definitions and classification of geographical information
Users	Municipalities, related organizations, companies and public

Table (4-6): Detailed definition of the systems

G. Basic databases

The basic databases needed for this program are as follows:

* Office and staffs DB
* Financial DB
* Security DB
* Rules and regulation DB
* Gates
* Real estate DB
* Vehicles DB
* Archive of documents DB
* Urban services DB
* Urban transportation DB
* GIS
* Statistics DB

H. Information dissemination programs

One of the most important services in an e-city is preparing the accurate information on time for the right person daily. The seen programs related to this field are listed in table (4-7):

Program code	Program	Plan	Sub-plan	Plan's code
D7	Information dissemination field	Cultural services (D701)	Online cultural centers	D70101
			Online publication	D70102
			Online TV	D70103
			Online cultural information	D70104
			Online entertainment	D70105
		Tourism (D702)	Online tourist	D70200
			Historical places	D70301
			Municipality online	D70302

		Urban information dissemination (D703)	Urban information	D70303
			Business information	D70304
			Trades information	D70305
			Official organization information	D70306
		Urban connectivity (D704)	Municipality on-line	D70401
			City council	D70402
			City on-line	D70403
		Safety and security (D705)	Police on-line	D70501
			Firefighting	D70502
			Health care	D70503
		Urban transportation (D706)	Online transportation services	D70601
			Inter cities trips on-line services	D70602

Table (4-7): Related programs

4-12-1 The plans of electronic city of Mashed

List of plans in e-city of Mased are shown in table (4-8):

Plan's name : on-line cultural centers
Plan's target : creating an on-line DB
Plan's range : cultural centers of the city Cultural centers programs Cinema and theater Ticket reservation

Plan's duties : creating a powerful DB
Prerequisite : information dissemination companies identity Benchmarking Feasibility study of the existing systems
Benefits for the city: municipality management development
Benefits for the citizens: Easy accessibility Time and cost saving
Undertaker : municipality
Teammate : Cultural centers
Plan's name : On-line publishing
Plan's target : Creating a publication DB
Plan's range: Mashed's journals Mashed's daily papers The city publications On-line delivery
Plan's duties : Creating powerful DBs
Prerequisite : Papers and magazines recognition Benchmarking the best patterns Feasibility of the existing systems
Benefits for the city: More income for the city
Benefits for the citizens: 24/7 accessibility Easy access Time and cost saving People's awareness
Undertaker : municipality

Teammate : publication companies
Plan's name : TV and radio on-line
Plan's target : On-line programs
Plan's range : Radio information TV information
Plan's duties : Creating powerful systems and networks
Prerequisite : Identity of on-line systems Identity of the necessary infrastructure Benchmarking Feasibility of the existing systems
Benefits for the city: World accessibility to the city TV and radio programs
Benefits for the citizens: On-line access
Undertaker :municipality
Teammate : radio and TV organization
Plan's name : On-line cultural information
Plan's target : Creating DB
Plan's range : Customs information Historical information
Plan's duties : Creating related DB
Prerequisite …
Benefits for the city: Tourist attraction
Benefits for the citizens: Peoples awareness attraction

Undertaker : Municipality
Teammate :Islamic culture organization
Plan's name : City spots on-line
Plan's target : Performing necessary information
Plan's range: City spots Urban facility spots Training and education spots Business centers Cultural centers Health care centers Sport spots Religious spots
Plan's duties : More and easy accessibility to different spots of the city
Prerequisite : City DB
Benefits for the city: City development and better planning for the city
Benefits for the citizens: Easy accessing to the city locations and spots
Undertaker : Municipality
Teammate : Both public and private sector
Plan's name :on-line municipality
Plan's target : Citizen's accessibility to the municipality information and increasing citizen's partnership and highlighting the municipality's capabilities
Plan's range : Municipality and all its departments and zones and staffs and management
Plan's duties : Performing the newest programs and decisions or rules and regulations

Prerequisite :   Preparing necessary documentation
Benefits for the city: Reduction on the number of the citizens' trips to municipality
Benefits for the citizens: Up to date information
Undertaker :   Municipality
Teammate :   Municipality organizations
Plan's name :   On-line urban information
Plan's target :   Performing necessary information about public situations
Plan's range :   City managers   City representatives   City map   History   City calendar   Weather and climate   Environment   Found and lost properties   City statistics reports
Plan's duties :   Information classification   Information updates   search
Prerequisite :   Feasibility study and priority definition
Benefits for the city: Stability of the city situation as an information base
Benefits for the citizens: More and easy accessibility
Undertaker :   Municipality
Teammate :   Private sector

Plan's name : On-line business information
Plan's target : Electronic commerce development
Plan's range : Trends, bids, auctions, stock markets …
Plan's duties : Easy accessibility to business information
Prerequisite : Databases
Benefits for the city: More investment and partnership and income
Benefits for the citizens: Easy and safe business
Undertaker : Municipality
Teammate : Companies and stock markets
Plan's name :official organizations
Plan's target : Easy and fast accessibility to the official organizations
Plan's range : All the governmental organization
Plan's duties : Performing a powerful search engine
Prerequisite : Creating DB for the governmental organizations
Benefits for the city: …
Benefits for the citizens: Time and cost saving More awareness
Undertaker : Municipality
Teammate : Governmental organizations
Plan's name : On-line city council

Plan's target :   Interaction between the city council and citizens
Plan's range :   City council
Plan's duties :   interaction
Prerequisite :   Accurate time scheduling of the city council representatives
Benefits for the city: Better decision making process   Fast and wide interaction with citizens
Benefits for the citizens: Effective planning
Undertaker :   Municipality
Teammate :   City council
Plan's name :police on-line
Plan's target :   Creating police DB
Plan's range :   Police information   Security   Rules and regulation
Plan's duties :   Creating powerful database
Prerequisite :   ….
Benefits for the city: Insecurity reduction
Benefits for the citizens: Safer society
Undertaker :   Municipality
Teammate :   police
Plan's name :   Health on-line

Plan's target : Creating health care DB
Plan's range : Emergency departments and health monitoring stations
Plan's duties : Creating a powerful network
Benefits for the city: A happy and healthy city
Benefits for the citizens: Healthy citizens and 24/7 accessibility to the medical services
Undertaker :municipality
Teammate :health care centers

Table (4-8): The plans of electronic city of Mashed

4-13 The relation between current and future urban goals and the vision of e-city of Mashed in the 5 year program of the city

This relation is shown in table (4-9)

Goal Vision		upgrading urbanization indexes	Improvement the urban environment	Improving the urban transportation	Urban security	Cultural affairs	Increasing partnership	Encouraging the culture of control	Upgrading social and cultural affairs	Reforming the official and final structure	Establishing coordinating in the management system
e-government vision	Knowledge base economy										
	Creating information society										
	Qualified life										

Goal		upgrading urbanization indexes	Improvement the urban environment	Improving the urban transportation	Urban security	Cultural affairs	Increasing partnership	Encouraging the culture of control	Upgrading social and cultural affairs	Reforming the official and final structure	Establishing coordinating in the management system
Vision											
e-city vision	Better services										
	A world class city										
	Competitive environment										
	Traffic reduction										
Municipality vision	Citizen oriented management										
	24/7 services										
	Quality guarantee of services										
	Sustainable revenue										
	Process clarification										
e-citizen vision	Information society citizen										

Table (4-9): The relation between current and future urban goals and the vision of e-city of Mashed

4-14 The matrix of relations between domains and visions in e-city of Mashed

This matrix has been shown in table(4-10)

Domain		Infrastructure	hardware	Training	Rules and regulation	Financial resources
Vision	Code	D1	D2	D3	D4	D5
e-government vision	Knowledge oriented economy			*		*
	Creating information society	*			*	
	Qualified life			*	*	
e-city vision	Better services	*	*			
	A world class city	*	*		*	
	Competitive environment		*		*	*
	Traffic reduction			*	*	
Municipality vision	Citizen oriented in management			*		
	24/7 services	*	*		*	
	Quality guarantee of services		*		*	
	Sustainable revenue					*
	Process clarification				*	
e-citizen vision	Information society citizen			*		

Table (4-10): The matrix of relations between domains and visions in e-city of Mashed

4-15 The matrix of domains and strategies in e-city of Mashed

In table (4-11) you can see this matrix:

Strategies / Domains	Information infrastructure development	Intelligent supervision on urban services upgrading	Training the citizens about e-services	Integrating the systems	more revenue for the city by applying IT	Reviewing the current procedures and improving them	Upgrading the quality, the services, the staffs and training	Creating urban databases
Infrastructure	*							
Hardware	*							
Training	*	*	*					*
Rules and regulations		*		*		*	*	
Financial resources		*			*			*
systems		*		*		*	*	
Cultural services	*	*					*	
Tourism	*	*					*	
Urban information dissemination	*	*					*	
Safety services	*	*					*	
Urban transmission		*					*	
Urban connectivity	*	*					*	

Table (4-11): The matrix of domains and strategies in e-city of Mashed

4-16 The matrix of domains and visions in e-city of Mashed, information domain

In table (4-12) the matrix of domains and visions based on information domain is shown:

Domain / vision		Cultural services					tourism	Urban information						Urban connectivity services			Safety services			Urban transportation	
Plan		Cultural center	publications	Radio and TV	Cultural information	On-line entertainment	On-line tourism	Urban spots	Online municipality	City on-line	Business information	Trades on-line	Governmental organization	Online municipality	City council on-line	City on-line	Police on-line	Firefighting	Online health care	Urban transportation	Inter cities transportation
code		D70101	D70102	D70103	D70104	D70105	D70200	D70301	D70302	D70303	D70304	D70305	D70306	D70401	D70402	D70403	D70501	D70502	D70503	D70601	D70602
e-government vision	Knowledge oriented economy					*	*													*	*
e-government vision	Creating information society	*	*	*	*	*	*	*	*	*	*	*	*	*	*	*	*	*	*	*	*
e-government vision	Qualified life	*	*	*	*	*								*	*	*	*	*	*	*	*
e-city vision	Better services	*	*	*	*	*											*	*	*	*	*
e-city vision	A world class city	*	*	*	*	*					*						*	*	*	*	*
e-city vision	Competitive environment						*				*										

Domain		Cultural services					tourism	Urban information						Urban connectivity services			Safety services			Urban transportation	
Plan		Cultural center	publications	Radio and TV	Cultural information	On-line entertainment	On-line tourism	Urban spots	Online municipality	City on-line	Business information	Trades on-line	Governmental organization	Online municipality	City council on-line	City on-line	Police on-line	Firefighting	Online health care	Urban transportation	Inter cities transportation
code / vision		D70101	D70102	D70103	D70104	D70105	D70200	D70301	D70302	D70303	D70304	D70305	D70306	D70401	D70402	D70403	D70501	D70502	D70503	D70601	D70602
Municipality vision	Traffic reduction	*	*			*		*	*	*	*	*	*	*	*	*					
	Citizen oriented in management													*		*					
	24/7 services													*	*	*					
	Quality guarantee of services																				
	Sustainable revenue																				
	Process clarification													*	*	*					
e-citizen vision	Information society citizen																				

Table (4-12): The matrix of domains and visions in e-city of Mashed, information domain

4-17 The matrix of domains and visions in e-city of Mashed, system domain

In table (4-13) the matrix of domains and visions in e-city of Mashed featured with system domain is shown:

Plan's domain	Code	e-government vision		e-city vision		
		Knowledge oriented economy	Creating information society	Qualified life	Better services	A world class city
GIS	D62000		*			
MIS	D61900		*			
Integrated library	D61800		*			
Real estate	D61600		*		*	
Training	D61500		*		*	
Project control	D61400	*	*			
Documentation	D61300		*			
Tariff	D61200		*			
Transportation	D60900		*		*	
Traffic control	D60800		*		*	
Ticket payment	D60700		*		*	
Taxation	D60600		*		*	
Light train system	D60500		*		*	
Urbanization system	D60400			*		
Electronic commerce	D60300	*	*	*	*	*
Urban services	D60200		*		*	
Integrated official system	D60100		*		*	

Competitive environment		*																
Competitive environment																		
Traffic reduction		*			*	*												
Citizen oriented in management																		
24/7 services	*		*				*	*	*	*				*	*			
Quality guarantee of services	*	*	*	*	*	*	*	*	*	*	*	*	*	*	*	*	*	*
Sustainable revenue		*																
Process clarification	*	*	*	*	*	*	*	*	*	*	*	*	*	*	*	*	*	*
Information society citizen																		

e-municipality vision / e-citizen vision

Table (4-13): The matrix of domains and visions in e-city of Mashed, system domain

Chapter 5

REMARKABLE RESULTS

Implementing the master plan of creating e-city of Mashed based on the municipality will have a lot of effects on economy, education and social matters of the city and citizens. What is really important here is an accurate and logical move towards the strategic macro plans in implementing e-city of Mashed. At first it is necessary to establish the strategic steering committee. This committee or we better say council's most important duty is to coordinate the executive projects in the field of e-city of Mashed. On the other hand it should act as a cathalizer among the private and public sectors.

At the same time cultural awareness among citizens and urban management can attract their partnership in this project and will prepare them for living and working in an e-society.

By applying IT in the society the city will be gifted with a lot of opportunities which are precious from the following point of views:

Economic point of view:

* Less expensive services
* Increasing in foreign and domestic investment
* Increasing economic deals between Mashed and its national and international neighborhood
* Tourist attractions
* e-banking development
* e-cards development

Social point of views:

* Online services 24/7
* Citizen's satisfaction

* Fast, easy and less expensive services
* Saving time and cost
* Corruption reduction
* Increasing social transaction
* Fair service distribution
* Air pollution reduction
* Job opportunities
* Increasing digital literacy
* International reputation

Cultural points of views:

* Process and procedures clarification
* On time, fast and qualified information dissemination
* Virtual training on urban problems
* Digital Medias
* Digital libraries
* On line pilgrimage

Political point of views:

* More international reputation and communication
* More political reputation as a pioneer city in this field among developing countries

One of the most important problems that the master plan has faced is the financial dimension of it. Since ICT projects are actually expensive and on the other hand they can affect the economical, political and social life of the people so, both public and private sector have some beneficial and non beneficial reactions on this matter. In order to solve this problem, especially encouraging the public sector on this project can be a great help, of course the effective factors on non governmental investment in this field should also be listed and solved as soon as possible, some of these effective factors are:

1-Investment security
2-Political and economical stability
3-IT
4-Economy situation and monitory system

Considering the pioneer countries and their experiences in IT applications we can deterministically confirm that in order to creating and developing IT the government must invest widely on IT and ICT infrastructures otherwise the objectives will never come to reality. Since the macro policies of the country is not always very clear the investors are interested in small and medium size projects which is another important problem in the country. Considering the national ICT documents will clear that annual governmental investment on e-government, e-healthcare, EC and e-learning are 4, 17, 6, and 60 dollars per person.

ICT credit allocation in the country's five year program is shown in table (5-1):

Macro plans	Public sector (billion rials)	Private sector's share
ICT development	120.2	50%
e-government	10.8	20%
e-learning	9.6	30%
e-healthcare	9.2	60%
EC	14.4	80%
Post development	1.5	20%
Sum of credits	174.7	

Table (5-1): ICT credit allocation

Based on this information, table (5-2) is predicted for e-city of Mashed with the population of 2.5 millions:

Macro plans	Public sector (billion rials)	Private sector's share
ICT development	5	50%
e-government	0.415	20%
e-learning	0.37	30%
e-healthcare	0.354	60%
EC	0.554	80%
Post development	0.58	20%
Sum of credits from the countries ICT budget	6.75	

Table (5-2): Predicted table

Another rival problem which can be a research for those who are interested in this field is the 4th step of implementing an e-city means integrating step. Almost none of the e-cities in the world have met this step completely so the cost of integrating step is unpredictable. The annual investment for implementing e-government in a country is different with others for example in England it is

200 pounds while in Iran it is just 4 $. This horrible gap shows that predicting costs in this field is not easy. For a city like Mashed it is suggested to define the projects priorities first with considering the costs. Anyway starting the project with the annual 4$ per person is the reference credit for this project and means just $10 million for 2.5 million citizens of Mashed.

PART TWO

Web-based urbanization integrated system

Chapter 6

INTRODUCTION

At the end of 1999 the subject" changing in the management of the munici-palities' organization and management in the country through IT and its appli-cations" became hot. The internet fever, MIS designing and different visions in municipalities' organizations ceased to some messed up programs in this field. Having uniform systems will prevent overlapping, redundancy and save costs. Existing a total but complete scheme will prevent illogical tasks and since the main duty of the municipalities are defining and creating services for the citizens to live in a secure, fair and well condition society, it is obvious that they are not away from the urban plannings. Their most important concern is implementing them and defining a proper framework and applying IT and ICT toward these meeting goals. The main goal of this part and implementing the integrated web based urbanization system is performing better services for the citizens, facilitating the ease of accessibility to the necessary information resources, establishing an effective urban management, getting coordinated with governmental organization to perform better services and help country's ICT development plan in order to putting e-government into reality.

Establishing an e-organization and managing IT in the municipalities will draw new methods in management and urban planning. This project acts as a cathalizer for creating macro plans of the cities. This plan consists of macro designing of software systems, macro designing of telecommunication infra-structures for mechanizing the urbanizations process and related services; it also consists of technical and economical feasibility studies and performing executive strategies. Macro designing means designing with covering the neces-sities. For example in software system's macro deigning, the systems and their capabilities and missions will be mentioned. By macro designing of telecom-munication infrastructures, the datacenters and their locations, their type of communications, speed and the communication network layers and totally network designing in order to defining hardware costs will be concerned.

e-city of Mashed and urbanization integrated system together establish a new management infrastructure which will finally cease to redefining the management structure. One of the advantages which will happen is pivoting the urban management in municipality. Planning the organization architecture is considered as an executive methodology in this master plan.

Planning the organization architecture consists of the municipalities' information architecture, applying architecture programs, internal network and infrastructure architecture, defining functional project and their priorities.

Urbanization information is one of the most exclusive systems in municipalities. 85% of the municipality income is gained through this system.70% of the physical citizen's referral to the municipality is related to this organization. So, urbanization organizations in any municipality are very important.

Establishing the new information and functional systems in municipalities means increasing the system's efficiency in gathering, classifying, processing the information, issuing necessary documents, following them and optimizing the facilities, potentials and protecting citizen's security. This master plan has a large amount of capabilities; it not only reduces the vast volume of tasks but also supports the citizen's rights.

6-1 Problem definition

One of the most important departments in a municipality is the urbanization and architecture department. This department consists of the most complex job processes and returnees.

As mentioned before 80 % of the municipalities revenue is provided by this department so it is a strategic department in the municipality and it is a good location for measuring the citizen's satisfaction of the municipality services. Verity of requests and complexity of the process, verity of executive instructions, different compiles, outward communications, job dependency to employees, lack of certifications, lack of the management accessibility to the up-to-date information and reports and so on are all the problem bottlenecks in municipalities. The existing situation and the management and personnel's attempt to attract the citizen's temporarily satisfaction is a barrier for solving these problems from the root. The urbanization department has offices in different city zones but each has its own charts. Some about 4-15 personnel are working in each of these departments and their main duties are as follows:

1-Issuing constructions licenses

2-Issuing evidences (warranties)

3-Following the constructions trespasses

The followings are different units of the mentioned departments in different zones of the city in municipality of Mashed:

1-Record and file formation unit

2-Expert unit

3-Topography unit

4-Planning and programming unit

5-Technical control unit

6-Permission issuing unit

7-License issuing unit

8-Trepasses surveying unit

9-Archive unit

6-2 Significance and feasibility

Urbanization integrated system's goal is enhancing a complete automation in municipality and information conveying for the 3 levels in urban information pyramid. This system is a complete set of integrated systems like urbanization, renovation, trades, estate, supervisor engineers, enforcing commands and GIS.

The aim of designing and implementing this system is providing a functional environment for different departments of the municipality and creating application programs. In other words this system is alive and can learn and by changing the environmental situations, it can adapt and grow with the help of system program maker which is an important part of the system. This capability will make the system independent from individuals and staffs' maintenance and the users can develop whatever they need with the lowest price and ease. The details of this subsystem are listed in the following chapters.

Chapter 7

VIEW FOUNDATIONS

7-1 Introducing IT types through a practical view

Applying lexis like IT, IS, OA has been common these days, even applying the word "internet" has become common these days. Let's explain these words and their relations with each other. The goal is producing a common language over IT and its applications.

7-1-1 Public ISs

Information system is a set of elements which are responsible for gathering, processing, storing, analyzing and distributing the information based on the right requests. Any system has input and output, proper inputs for an information system are: data, statistic information, opportunities, threats, instructions etc and output consists different reports, information, analyzing procedures and graphs etc.Any information system processes on inputs and produces outputs. These results can be sent to the users or even be used as input for the other systems. They also can be used as feedback for the same system. Like any system an information system interacts with its environment. Information systems can be manual or mechanized.

Formal and informal information systems

Like any other systems an information system can be either formal or informal. The formal systems can define procedures, their input or output forms are standard and have fixed definitions. Informal systems can change their forms and size. The important point is to recognize them. They can affect the staffs or even the formal systems. They can even act an important role in complaint or encouragement of the area they are involved.

7-1-2 Computer based public ISs

These are systems that use computers to do a part or the whole of their tasks. A computerized information system may consist of new PCs and software or thousands of computers with hundreds of printers, plotters and other network equipments and databases. The fundamental elements of any information system are listed below, and of course it should be mentioned that not all computerized information systems consist them all:

- Hardware
- Software
- Database
- Network
- Procedures
- Users
- Objectives
- Social concepts

7-1-3 Technology relationships with ISs

In a simple definition, information technology is a technologic view to an information system. Information technology consists of hardware, DB, software and other related things. Scientists and experts in the field of information systems and information technology have looked differently to these concepts. Sometimes they are on this idea that IT is a subset of IS and sometimes they believe that IT is integrated with IS, in some books IT is considered as a concept with more wide meaning of IS and holds some information systems by itself.

7-1-4 IS classification

Information systems are classified in different ways. The most important classification types are based on the organizations levels or fields of supports.

A. Classification base on the organization levels

Any organization has its departments, offices and zones. Most of the organizations have staff's department, financial office, accounting and public affairs part. They send their reports to other levels. This hierarchical multilevel structure is common and traditional.

Away from organizing information system is providing them base on these structure. So, the information system can be prepared for the departments and functional parts and even for a special task. These subsystems can be related or separated. System designers can design these systems centralized or decentralized based on the organization needs.

B. Classification base on the activity field

In this classification, the information systems are divided based on the field and type of the organization's activity. For example the basic information systems based on the organization's activity in municipalities are as follows:
* Payroll system
* Finance and accounting system
* Contractors accounting system
* Budget system
* Technical services system
* Warehouses system
* Transportation system
* Service activities management information system
* Properties system
* Office automation system
* Information dissemination system
* Urbanization and renovation system
* Logistic system
* Taxation system for vehicles
* Taxation system for factories and trades

In any field of activity there are some basic daily tasks which can be done by computer and put into an information system framework. It should be mentioned that any field of activity may need more than one of the information systems for example payroll system, personnel system, accounting system are all in the financial field.

C. Classification based on the type of system's support

The third method of classification is based on the type of the system's support. For example an information system can support all staffs duties in functional level where ever they work. Similarly managers can use the system facilities without considering their field of activities. The famous systems of this type are:
* TPS
* MIS
* OA

* DSS
* EIS
* Intelligent support systems

7-1-5 The relationship between IS and internet

Some of the most common services on internet are: www, e-mail, FTP, chatting, Usenet and Telnet.

World wide web and for short www is a service with world's standards for storing, retrieving, forming and performing information. Its structure is client server and all multimedia facilities are accessible through this. It is based on HTML.e-mail is the most famous service on internet and is used not only for personal tasks but for research and commercial purposes. FTP is a service for receiving and transferring files. Chat is in fact a virtual meet or talk.Usenet provides a group discussion on the internet, people can find the discussion they are interested in through bulletin boards and take part.Telnet is a service that enables you to connect to your own computer at home or office when you are away.

Now after a short description for the most famous internet services lets point to the internet facilities in the organization. If we divide the organizations relations into 2 groups means inward relations and outward relations, the inward relations in an organization are done through TPS, MIS, OAS, DSS and EIS but in outward relations internet itself is very useful. Of course internet is useful in both inward and outward of the organization relations so, from now on we call it full communication.

7-1-6 IT professional spectrum

Variety of IT teams are necessary in order to applying IT in an organization like system designers, analyzers, programmers, network managers, database managers, web designers, network security professionals etc. these teams can work together and implement IT in the organization.

7-2 IT applications in municipality management

Generally IT can be used in any organization almost into separated field namely internet and information system or for short IS. Applying IS in an organization is shown in figure (7-1):

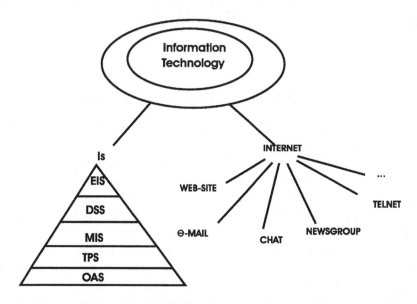

Figure (7-1): Applying IS in an organization

Of course the above scheme can be more specific for the municipalities as shown in figure (7-2):

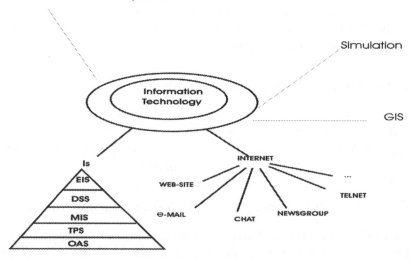

Figure (7-2): Applying IS in municipalities

A. Internet applications in municipalities

The benefit of internet is obvious for everybody. The extra high speed growth rate of internet in the world and in Iran is inevitable. Municipalities have already been delayed in this field. Lots of cities in developing countries even don't have a public website. But in developed countries like America almost all the cities large or small at least have their own websites which are very useful. Most of the cities services are accessible over the internet. By performing a sample proto-type for municipalities websites(portals) not only there will be a cost reduction on web designing but also variety types of urban services will be defined and the supporting, up-grading and maintaining will be done easily. The computer services union in municipalities' organizations in Iran are working on it.

Based on a wide study on the cities websites (studying more than 70 selected websites from 250 options) and analyzing their contents comparing with the municipalities' concerns, the following dendriform is suggested as icons in a sample prototype:

1. Public information
2. Entertainment
3. Transportation
4. Social affairs
5. Security in city
6. Emergency phone numbers
7. Urban improvement
8. Urban affairs
9. Climates and weather
10. Environment
11. Urban health
12. Urban training
13. Unexpected accidents
14. My city
15. Municipality taxation system
16. Urban counseling
17. FAQs
18. Programs
19. City council
20. Municipality organizations
21. Countries' municipalities
22. Contact with urban professionals
23. Contact with other e-cities

B. IS application in municipalities

Information systems are applied vastly in municipalities. In this wide area there are accounting systems, office automation systems, urbanization and renovation system, project management system and many others.

7-3 Introducing the web based urbanization integrated system as an exclusive system for the municipalities

As mentioned before the urbanization department in Iranian's municipalities are very important and critic because it is a complex department with micro details of its subsystems. The source of some about 85% of the revenue in municipality of Mashed is provided by this important department. 70% of those who set out for the municipality is related this department. The goals of establishing the new information and functional system in municipalities are: More efficiency in gathering, classifying, processing, functioning and accounting data and information and more effectiveness in issuing types of documents and certifications, optimized usage and allocation of staffs and resources with protecting and supporting the citizen's rights.

A proper information system must be able to answer and satisfy different types of citizens' request like:

1. Facilitating the official and functional tasks of the organization
2. Satisfying the citizens
3. Preventing the overlapping and data redundancy
4. Deleting the unnecessary papers from the records and archives
5. Capability of gathering, processing the necessary information from the files
6. Gathering, classifying and processing the financial information of the organization
7. Performing office automation
8. Creditors and debtors accounts
9. Performing management information services
10. Performing classified management information
11. Performing functional and informational services for other official departments

It is clear that based on the ministry of interior the web based urbanization system must have a lot of capabilities, each of the above items can be discussed widely. Municipalities are aware of the importance of these items. They knew that through execution of this system there will be a reduction in the volumes of their tasks. For further information let's get more familiar with this system from two separated aspects as follows:

A. Capabilities

1-File creating process

This process is one of the most important ones but it is time consuming in urbanization departments. Right now the file creating process is different in renovation department from the urbanization department. This process is more critics in the first department.

Through this master plan these two file creation process will be integrated and done more accurate. These two different departments can use their common information interchangeably. Through implementing this system just the needed papers and documents will be recorded so this system is gifted for better regulations and can be considered as a good pattern for other organization.

2-Inspecting estate process

This step is very important for urban issuing papers. The current inspecting process of estates causes a lot of troubles during the follows of the files in the municipalities. Through this new system the inspecting forms will be filled through an accurate structure and all necessary information will be gathered for the others who need them. So repeated returns which exist right now will be dropped and the citizen's rights will be guaranteed.

3-The defining of constructions infringement process

This part is a professional sector the reports of these departments can be sent for determining the amount of infringement and sending it automatically to the proper commissions e-mail boxes.

4-Issuance of vote

The proper position for this part is receiving the file by computer, studying it and looking up for a fraud and assurance a vote and sending the file for the other part of process.

5-Carrying out orders process

All the necessary functions in this section like approving the votes, serving citizens with a notice, following the orders executions and preparing the reports will be done automatically by computers through the web based urbanization integrated system of the municipality of Mashed.

6-Taxation process

All the accountings in this part will be done based on the rules and regulations automatically. Accurate and fast accountings of taxes and issuing fines straight and clear without different compiles are the benefits of the system on this matter.

7-Issuing buildings identification process

Actually by applying the new system in municipality some experts believe that the traditional system will be useless because on that system all information about the buildings would be gathered manually which is useless in the new system. Municipalities are even able to transfer the data and information of the buildings on citizen's e-cards. Considering the improvement of IT in urbanization's systems and its penetration on inward and outward correspondence, all possible corresponding with necessary information items to insert in and the right number of carbon copies and the name of receivers are predicted in the system. This capability makes the processes of tasks much easier than before.

8-Answering process

All the municipality's customers will receive their requested information fast and easy.

9-New urbanization systems

The new urbanization systems must be designed the way that they are able to store not only the special information for the special files but the information needed to operate on the file all in detailed and visible and follow able.

10-Files move

Through this capability studying the file for determining the next destination is not needed any more and the files move exactly where they must automatically.

11-Archive

Through the new system this part will face a great change.

12-Management and monitoring

In this system there will be proper monitoring system for managers in different levels.

13-System information management

In this new system a powerful MIS is needed the main task of this part is producing verity of complete and classified reports based on the approved and legal requests. These reports can be used as good tools for making plans or reengineering tasks or even measuring the staffs' functions more effectively.

B. Capability of documents reduction

The urbanization and renovation department in any municipality faces a high density of paper documents and it is because of the nature of what they do. It is noticeable that this system doesn't force the users in their paper reduction but it try to change this culture with the present culture gradually.

A file in urbanization department may consist more than 100 papers, in renovation department the number and importance of the documents are less than the urbanization department by implementing the new system all the documents in renovation department can be completely detected so, there will be no physical archive for them and in urbanization department 50 % of documents can be dropped by implementing the system completely and almost 50 % of the archive needed now will be reduced. In other words all documents that municipality is not directly involved in them will be deleted and the municipality will just store the documents which are necessary.

C. Centralized information system

These systems are set of computerized systems with powerful databases for gathering, classifying and processing the urban information. These systems are classified into 3 hierarchical categories:

First: Centralized database of urbanization system

Second: Gathering, organizing and applying system for urbanization and renovation department in any provinces.

Third: Gathering, organizing and applying system for urbanization and renovation departments in the whole country and ministry of interior.

Chapter 8

SAMPLE SOCIETY AND THE RESEARCH TOOL

8-1 Existing situation of urbanization organization in municipality of Mashed

The basic unit in a municipality is its urbanization department. It is complex and as mentioned it is a financial resource for the municipality so, it is obvious that it is a critic department and practically is a place for measuring the citizen's satisfaction from the municipality's services. Variety of requests and complexity of their functional process and variety of instructions, compilers, tasks dependencies, lack of documents and management access to the information and update reports are all factors which can put municipalities in trouble. Right now the urbanization department in different zones of the municipality of Mashed is under the control of urbanization deputy. Unfortunately this dependency itself has its own problems. For example there is not a unique chart for it in its different offices in different zones of the city. The main tasks of this part are:

1-Issuing contracts licenses

2-Issuance evidences (warranties)

3-Following the constructions trepasses

The different units in urbanization departments in different zones of the municipality are:

1-File formation unit

2-Experts unit

3-Topology unit

4-Planning and programming unit
5-Technical control unit
6-Permission issuing unit
7-License issuing unit
8-Trepasses surveying unit
9-Archive unit

1-File formation unit

This unit is a critic one. The current process is requesting for a copy of documents, IDs etc from the citizens in order to forming their files. The current problems related to this unit are:

A. Incomplete information of staffs in order to guide the customers or giving them proper advices.

Most of the personnel who work in this part are not educated about their jobs. The citizens or we better say customers have to ask the others to help them which waste a lot of time.

B. Lack of classification of the requests

The citizen's requests must be verified which means receiving different information based on the requests. For example the request for issuing a license can be classified in the form of request for construction, renovation, development and repair etc.

2-Experts unit

In order to issuing different types of licenses and certifications the municipalities' experts in urbanization and architecture field will observe the estate or building which is an important and critic step for different point of views like corruptions, bribery, lack of uniform forms, wasting time and money.

3-Construction trepasses

Social problems like immigration, poverty, unemployment, illiteracy all and all cease to illegal constructions, by the way those who goes for the licenses, after getting these papers they ignore them. These problems will finally show themselves in urban deformations and by passing the time the shape and form of the city will differ from what was predicted at first. Based on some surveys the ambiguity in rules and regulations are another reasons for trepasses.Varieties of rules and regulations cease in differs of compiles, lack of transparency and finally differs in results and ignoring the municipality and the citizen's rights.

4. Archive

The problems related to archiving systems in the municipality are as follows:
A. More than one archive for any estates like urbanization archive, renovation archive and trades archives, this type of archiving is costly and time consuming
B. More than one files for a building
C. Lots of files and document
D. Dependency to personnel

5. Complexity in taxation accounting system

6. Not fast answering system

7. Insufficiency of urbanization management

8. Manual movement of the file

9. Insuffiency in statistic and managerial reports

10. Problems in execution the orders

8-2 Introducing web based urbanization integrated system

One of the aims of this system is moving toward a complete automation in municipalities and covering the necessary information for all three levels of the urban information pyramids. It is an integrated system and consists urbanization system, renovation system, trade system, supervisor engineers, execution of orders system and GIS. This system provides an environment for three levels of the municipality's pyramid accessibility to the information is shown in figure (8-1). Safe, proper and up to date infrastructures are the characteristics of the system. This system provides an operational environment for all the municipality departments. It is not just application software, this system is alive and can learn from the environment and different situations can be changed by its "programmer".This part helps the system to adapt itself with the environment. As mentioned before this capability make the system free of dependency to the staffs, the user can access to the system with ease and minimized cost.

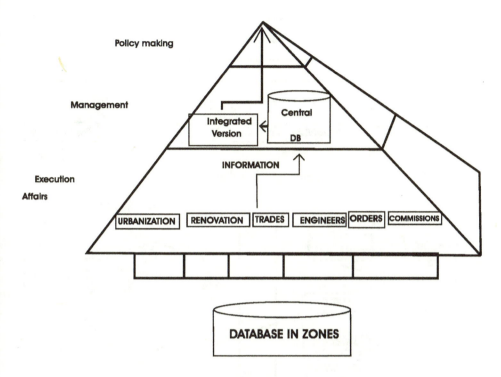

Figure (8-1): Web based urbanization integrated system

Total system connects the urbanization, renovation, trade and GIS, MIS and programmer systems together and provides a complete different software environment for the users. Its designing is based on the newest technologies in a way that a user as soon as he/she gets into the system can access the DB as much as it is defined for him or her, after doing the necessary functions on the file the next destination of the file will be automatically defined and the file will be sent for the next station. The subsystems are shown in figure (8-2). In figure (8-3) the connectivity among them is shown.

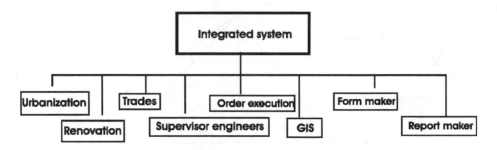

Figure (8-2): Subsystems

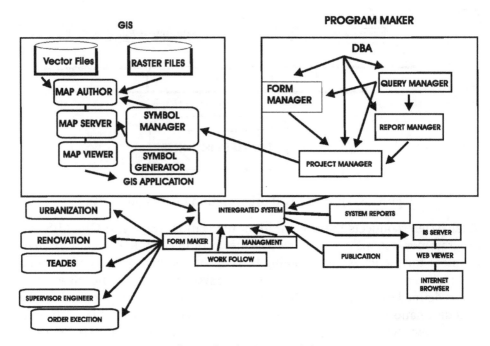

Figure (8-3): Connectivity

8-3 Characteristics of the system

The major characteristics of the web-based urbanization integrated system in e-city of Mashed are:

1-Task follows technology
2-Croquis grapher
3-Map album
4-Program maker

5-GIS

6-Dynamic organization chart defining

7-Intelligence detailed plan functions and operations by applying the plan's map

1-Applying task follow technology

By applying task follow technology the tasks follow among different units which are related to the total system are completely changed. The benefits of applying this technology are as follows:

A. Time reduction in transferring the files

In the web based integrated system file transfer will be done in a fraction of time while this process consumes 80 % of the total time now.

B. Task follows optimization

Any request in the system has a task follow. The system won't accept the requests without a defined task follow. This ceased to optimized task follow classification for those with task follow or without it. For those without task follow it will be defined.

C. Directing the file automatically

With the help of different task follows stored in the task follow databases and the entered information or produced information and other situations in the active file the system automatically directs the file to its next destination. So linear directing process of files which now exists would be meaningless and there will be a lot of time and cost savings. In figure (8-4) the next path method for the processing file with the task follow technology is shown:

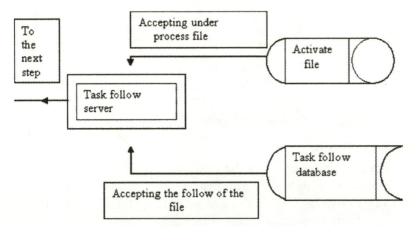

Figure (8-4): Path method for the processing file with the task follow technology

D. Process monitoring

This part of the system is designed in a way to be able to monitor and control the process follow of the file. With the help of this tool the urban managers will define the maximum stop in each unit so the civic staffs are supposed to do their jobs before ending the death time and by predicting the right time for the file's process from the start to end there will be costumer's satisfaction from the urban managers and finally the municipality.

E. Preventing the self opinions

The entire request in this system has a task follow which automatically would be executed on files. This process prevents the staff's self opinions on the file and the service would be fair for all.

F. Measuring the staff's function

This plan can be used as a tool for measuring the staff's function which is shown in figure (8-5):

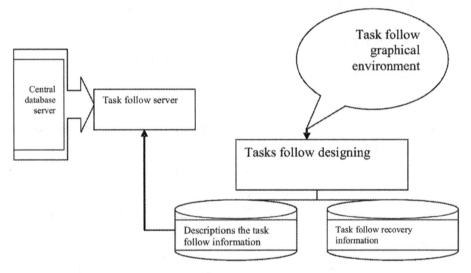

Figure (8-5): A tool for measuring the staff's function

2-Croquis grapher

This part of the system provides the possibility of drawing the estates croquis in an independent graphical environment. By the help of this subsystem all the maps can be drawn by scale and the reports are printable. Since the municipality faces a large amount of estates maps this system stores the croquis in a special format in a special database and call in them when necessary in other words the estates croquis will be no more stored pictorial.

This technology has had an effective affect on the speed of call in and call out the croquis. Another capability of this part is its library of sample and symbols. More than 2000 symbols are defined for this system. The relation among different parts of the system is shown in figure (8-6):

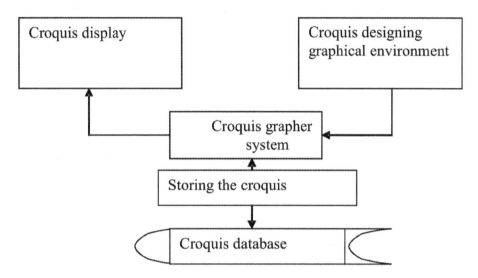

Figure (8-6): The relation among different parts of the system

The noticeable capabilities of the croquis grapher system are:
* Independent graphical environment
* Scales definition
* Croquis designing environment
* Croquis objects
* Defining the objects characteristics
* Symbols
* Moving the objects
* Advanced graphical capabilities
* Attaching text to the croquis
* Online characteristics definitions for the croquis
* Copying and transferring the objects to another file
* Printing
* Printing status definition
* Maximizing and minimizing the croquis
* Defining the characteristics of the designing page

3-System's map album

This album provides the possibility of storing and calling in the maps through Dwg. Dxf vectors. The maps are free from a especial plat form like Auto-CAD. The capabilities of this part are:

* Call in and call out the maps with vectoral format of Dwg and Dxf
* Turning on and off the maps layers
* Minimizing and maximizing
* Movement
* Rotating
*Attaching text
* Attaching shapes and object

4-System's program maker

Based on the daily up dates the urban management can adapt itself with this part of the system. System's program maker parts are:

* Project manager
* DB administrator
* Forms administrator
* Reports administrator
* Query administrator

Project manager

The capabilities of this part are:

* Sending and receiving the produced forms
* Applying database in projects
* Defining the starts forms of projects
* Defining the public variable for the project
* Project management

Database administration

Tables, indexes which are necessary in the project and the relations between tables with considering the necessary database can easily be defined. The most important in this part are:

* Creating, updating and even dropping databases
* Creating, updating and deleting databases' tables
* Creating, updating and deleting fields
* Defining the indexes for the table's fields
* Defining the candid keys for the tables
* Defining the relations between tables

Files administrator
This tool provides the possibility of creating forms both by designing and by wizard. The characteristics of this part are:
* Data entry forms
* Information observation forms
* Hybrid forms
* Source forms
* Tool bars
* Graphs
Even the designing environment has basic characteristics and capabilities like:
* Creating, updating, inserting, deleting labels
* Creating, updating, inserting, deleting text boxes
* Creating, updating, inserting, deleting lists
* Creating, updating, inserting, deleting receiving boxes
* Creating, updating, inserting, deleting buttons
* Creating, updating, inserting, deleting list boxes
* Creating, updating, inserting, deleting hierarchical structure
* Creating, updating, inserting, deleting printable lists
* Creating, updating, inserting, deleting frameworks
* Creating, updating, inserting, deleting images
* Creating, updating, inserting, deleting font, size and color
* Creating, updating, inserting, deleting the objects in the forms
* Creating, updating, inserting, deleting the tool bar
* Defining icons for he tool bar items
* Right, left and center justifying
Report management
This is a powerful tool in order to crate reports
The capabilities of this part are:
* Creating variety of reports related to tables
* Defining the size of the page
* Defining the fields and functions
Query management
This part provides the query options and its characteristics are:
* Creating different queries like select, up date, insert and delete
* Defining the limitations
* Defining the parameters
* Descending and ascending sorts
* Information classification
* Tables merging

* Arithmetic function definitions
* Query
* Preprinting the query

5-GIS

Geographic information system with the help of the newest software technologies offers a suitable environment to the users to create their maps, tables and forms easily and connecting them together. The capabilities of this system are:
* Increasing vectoral layers with pft, rat, dgn, anf, dwg and Dxf formats
* Inserting RASTER layers with jpg, bmp format
* Defining the layers characteristics
* Creating and adding different type of layers to the map
* Defining relation among created maps
* Creating shp layers
* Overlapping vectoral layers and raster layers and vice versa
* Defining and conveying regular geographical networks
* Storing the created maps
* Managing the entities of the system

The last item is a tool for creating special symbols for entities which are used in the system that by clicking on a symbol (icon) the user can get the proper information related to that symbol. This tool's capabilities are:
* Customizing a symbol
* Archive
* Defining the relation between the icon and the forms, reports, graphs
* Unlimited icon defining
* Unlimited icon distributions on the map
* Powerful tools for creating symbols and icons
* Different allocations of forms, reports and icons to an entity
* Searching system
* Measuring the distance between two or more points on the map
* Sending the map to the printer
* Sending the map by email

6-Dynamic organization chart definition

This part has been added to the users' management section and can define different users based on the organizational chart in graphical environment. This environment based on the defined chart and the type of accessibility will be defined.

7-Intelligence detailed plan functions and operations by applying the plan's map

The urbanization integrated system's input are the existing map and the detailed plan, the system can accept them separately and process on them.

8-4 Conveying a plan for e-city of Mashed architecture framework

Total organization architecture means that based on the experiences of other sciences it has proved that factors like dimensions, complexity, expandation and specific characteristics are the most important parameters in decision making on any type of architecture. Where ever designing a new entity or system is needed or the complexity of dimension goes far from the limitations the architecture will be needed. Both science and art are involved in the architecture. The organizational architecture faces a system that is conceptual and it is not tangible and the relations come out of the job cultures.

Architecture definition:
Providing a technical description from a system describes the phenomena structure of the system, the relations between them, the designing rules and the evaluation during the time. In summery we can say that the creation of total integrated organization is the basic factor in performing the organization, because they need information system development, special purpose MIS, all propose MIS with high flexibility against inward and outward pressures.

Architecture components
Flexibility in large systems occurs only if the components are reusable, reliable and are able to contact with each other. Organization architecture is a defined combination of fundamental phenomena which are mixed based on the missions and strategies of the organization. These fundamental elements are: information, process, location, staffs and motivation.

The difference between total organization architecture and the IS development technologies
Designing and producing small and local information system is not anything new there are a lot of experience and good background in this field like object oriented methods with the flexibility characteristics. The above methods are not applicable in large scale systems. These large scale systems need a total vision with considering all its aspects that connect these discrete systems.

Guidelines for conveying the pervasive architecture process

This is a four phase process
1. Start
* Providing the stack holders and suppliers trust
* Defining the management structure
* Attracting the middle management support
* Defining the path and methods
* Establishing the steering committee
* Defining the architecture plans management
2. Process definitions
* Architecture field
* Architecture depth
* Choosing suitable products for architecture
* Surveying and choosing a proper frame work
* Localizing the chosen frame work
* Proper architecture tool
3. Pervasive architecture development phase
* Defining the master models
* Defining the existing architecture
* Defining the desired architecture
* Defining the transferring plan
4. Implementation and maintaining phase
* Implementing the pervasive architecture
* Maintaining and up grading
The pervasive architecture frame work for e-city of Mashed
Developing and maintaining architecture is in fact a cycle. Pervasive architecture for e-city of Mashed concerns about know how, development and maintaining the pervasive architecture.
Framework in fact holds the contents which must develop not the content itself. This frame work in fact describes the development management methods. During surveying different methods on this matter especially FEAF some of the basic elements will be appeared which are as follows:
*Architecture forwarder
*Strategic direction
*Technical architecture
*Target architecture
*Architecture segmentation
*Architecture methods
*Architecture standards

Considering the above items from the FEAF point of view a four level framework appears that each level is a base for the next one.

Pervasive architecture frame work for e-city of Mashed

The basic thoughts for that architecture are the results of surveying FEAF, FEA, PSRM and ZACMAN. These basic frame works are the most famous ones. FEAF frame work is a special state of zacman; It has a complete and good documentation and is full of experiences. Selecting the proper frame work is one of the supervisor's architecture duties.

Localizing the selected framework

In order to localizing the mentioned framework the following points must be considered:

* Since these are references frameworks they should be customized
* Through customization the cultural and religional behaviors must be considered
* Transmission forwarders based on the countries and their cultures are different
* Other experiences in this field must be considered

As mentioned, the reference framework for defining the architecture frame work of Mashed has been FEAF and zacman after adapting them with the suggested model for e-city of Mashed. In figure (8-7) the suggested architecture framework for e-city of Mashed has been shown which is implementable in 3 levels, the total scheme of these 3 levels are in figures (8-8), (8-9) and (8-10).

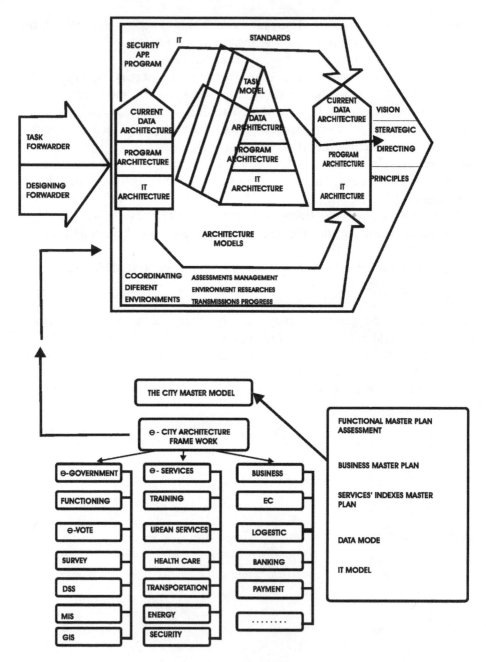

Figure (8-7): Suggested architecture frame work for e-city of Mashed

Level one:

This level is the top level in the pervasive architecture framework of e-city of Mashed. There are 8 effective elements in developing and maintaining the pervasive architecture of e-city of Mashed which will be discussed but before that in figure (8-8) the level one of the architecture has been shown and we see the direction of the movement which is from left to right and the architecture cycle.

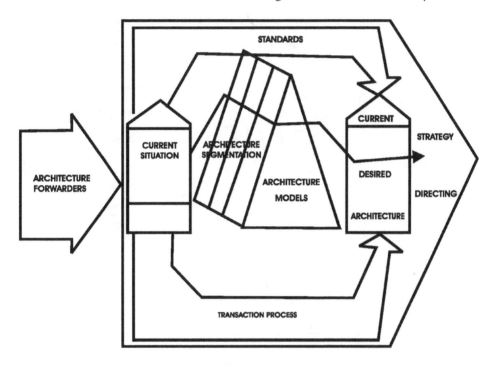

Figure (8-8): Level one

* Architecture forwarders
* Strategic direction
* Current architecture
* Target architecture
* Transmission process
* Architecture segmentation
* Architecture models
* Standards

Level 2

This level describes more details in comparing with the previous level. This level can be divided into 2 parts the upper part which shows the tasks field in the pervasive system and the lower part which shows the designing architecture and supports the defined tasks. The relationship between these two is e forwarder relation; The scheme of this part is shown in figure (8-9):

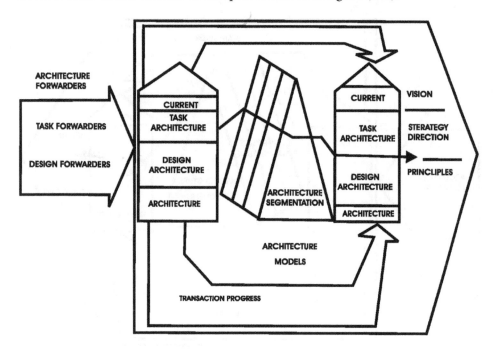

Figure (8-9): Level two

The components of this part are:
* Architecture forwarder
* Current architecture
* Target architecture
* Architecture models
* Architecture segmentation
* Strategic directions
Of course these elements are defined tailor-made for this level.

Level 3

This level of the architecture expands the designing architecture part which was mentioned in level 2 and shows the data architecture programs and technology architecture which is shown in figure (8-10):

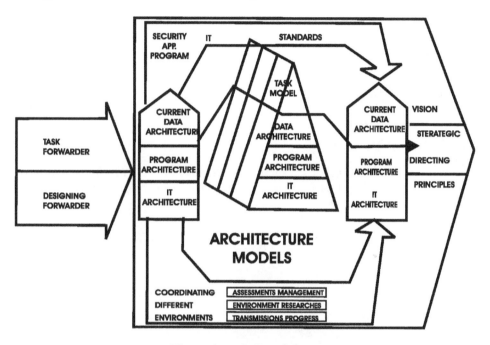

Figure (8-10): Level three

The important parts of this level are:

Current architecture for designing:
* Architecture for current date
* Architecture design for application program
* Architecture design for current technology
Target architecture design
* Architecture for data's target
* Architecture for application program's target
* Architecture for current technology's target
Designing model
* Data model
* Application programs model
* Technology model

Transmission process
* planning for investment
* reviewing the investment management
* Environmental research
* Fortune and finance management
* Logistic
* leading the architecture
Standards
* Security standards
* Data standards
* Application programs standards
* Technology standards

Level 4:

In this level the planning for pervasive architecture for e-city of Mashed will be defined, level 4 is the start point for the growth and supports of the business architecture.

Chapter 9

ANALYZING THE MODEL

9-1 The role of IT in a municipality

Man, money and machine are basic sources for producing goods but today another vital source has been added to these 3Ms, means information. This factor has directed the organization toward developing information management. In other words most of the organizations have come to this word that they must invest a lot of computerizing. So, in order to control and monitoring the costs of the organizing management information systems with the help of computer new policies, methods and executive paths are needed.

As mentioned municipalities have not been exceptions in this field and in order to being aware of their situation at a moment for making accurate decisions they need to use computerized systems. In the previous chapters you learned that municipalities' environments face changes all the time, so their system must be flexible enough to face different policies and to adapt themselves fast and right. Right now most of the municipalities don't own these systems or their systems are old fashioned and isolated, for example in most of the municipalities the real estates auditing systems are not integrated and they are like isolated islands. These systems stores the information which are gathered by physical observation of the estates and buildings and through using special formulas, indexes and tables they convert the information items into an estimated cost and finally the output will be the price and based on it the tax will be accounted and printed. When there are mass of files this manual process will be time and cost consuming.

Today with the help of IT powers the users are more capable. System's integrity will cease to more flexibility and can satisfy citizens. Today information can't be limited in other words managers have come to this truth that sharing information can solve their problems. Right now there is no connection among the current isolated information systems so, the most important problems in such systems are:

* Information transmission among different systems is impossible
* There are repeated information entries
* Incompatibility of information in a unique file
* Information conflation is impossible

In an integrated system all systems use a common database, these systems are flexible in providing reports and being updated.Integrated systems shares data and information easily through a DBMS. Global vision in designing databases will provide the logical connectivity of information from different sources. Through this vision when designing advanced systems the information pyramids of municipalities can be defined in 3 levels: executive affairs, management and policy making. The necessary information in each level is highly considered.

Figure (9-1) has shown this pyramid, the head of the pyramid are municipality's policy makers like city council or interior ministry, the middle level is for municipality's management and the base level is for the functional elements.

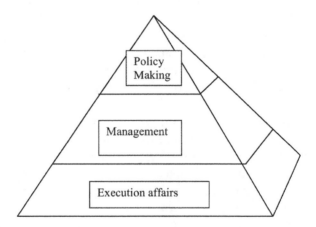

Figure (9-1): The information pyramids of municipalities can be defined in 3 levels: executive affairs, management and policy making.

At the summit of this pyramid defining rules and regulations and budgeting policies will be formed, the very detailed information is not necessary there. This policy will be formed to action plans in the middle level and the functional level which is in the base, executes these action plans. The information pyramid of the municipality has 3 dimensions; Information is involved in all 3 levels and is the base infrastructure in each level. The result of each level act as data entry (input) for the next level so their accuracy and up-to-dating is important for the accuracy of the next level.

The successful systems in municipalities are those which support all 3 levels in other words systems are designed based on the information requests. In functional level civic staffs tasks are directly involved in daily activities of a municipality and so are the released information. Their watchfulness in doing their duties is very precious for the other sectors. The improper information will cause a lot of problems for the others. For example when the auditing staffs call on the estates one by one and audit the estates then the information gathered with some other factors will help in calculating the taxes. All the necessary information will be gathered by the functional level but not all of them are necessary for the next level

Isolated systems and their role in the municipalities pyramid

The isolated information systems are designed for a single purpose they are not integrated and are not able to satisfy the information needs of the urban management. They can not be merged with other systems and feed the other levels needs of information.

9-2 Integrated systems and their role in urban information pyramid of Mashed

The characteristics of such a system that is shown in figure (9-2) are:

* Accuracy and reliability of the system in all levels

Since the system responses the functional level and the detailed necessary information for the executive sections are involved in this part it is obvious that the information are gathered carefully. This information will be used in the reports which can be requested by the managers in the middle level. These are accurate because they can be requested at a moment.

* Up-to-date information

* Flexibility

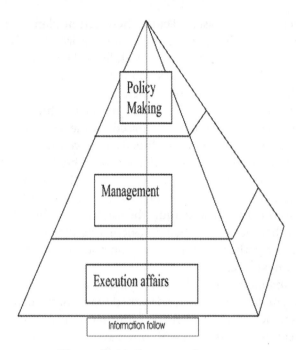

Figure (9-2): Integrated systems

9-3 Different parts of integrated system

Actually any integrated system is made up of different subsystems as follows:

9-3-1 Renovation subsystem

This sub system is an automation system for the necessary functions in this part like estate auditing calculating estate taxes, formally announcement and etc. It has 2 different versions here, one for each municipality's zone and one for the central organization of the municipality with capability of integrating. The duties of this one are providing necessary and up to date information for the different managerial levels in order to provide proper reports for them and facilitate their policy maker duties etc.

9-3-2 Trades sub systems

These subsystems automate the trade and business classes and like the others are provided in 2 versions.

9-3-3 Integrated version

This is a special version of the system for gathering information for urbanization and renovation tasks from files, and preparing suitable reports for the municipalities policy makers and also for the citizens that is shown in figure (9-3)

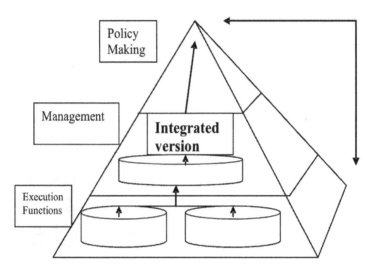

Figure (9-3): Integrated version

When the mentioned information gathered by the integrated version they will be processed and delivered in special formats for different urban managers and policy and decision makers. This integrated version will get in touch with other systems periodically and records the latest changes accurately. One of the capabilities of this integrated version is supporting the information dissemination for outward of the organization. The produced information in this part can be a good source for other organizations which can be received by them through accessing the web based municipality urbanization integrated system's database, some of these organizations are:

- Information and telecommunication company
- Real estates
- Registering offices
- Urban lands
- Gas and oil organization
- Energy organization

9-4 Describing the subsystems in web-based integrated urbanization system of the municipality of Mashed

The total system consists:

- Urbanization
- Renovation
- Trades
- Task follow
- Croquis grapher
- Map's album
- Supervisors engineers
- GIS
- Program maker

The relationships among the above systems are shown in figure (9-4):

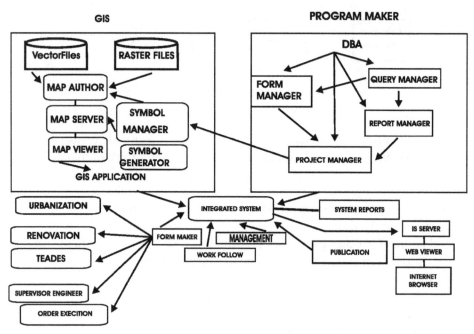

Figure (9-4): The relationships among the mentioned systems

1-Urbanization
The major duties in this sub system consist of the followings:
A. Responding
Personal answering
There is a part in this integrated system with the name of answering the requests there is a computer which is connected to the total system. Responding to a file is very fast and easy in this part.
Remote answering
- Answering through municipality's portal
- Answering through email
- Answering through fax

B. File formation
- Structure modification in file formation department
- Simplicity of the process
- Requests classification
- Documents reduction
- Independency from personnel's memories
- One-step file formation

C. Observation
One of the most important steps in issuing licenses is the reports of the experts observations, these observes are not only important but very sensitive and usually causes misunderstandings and problems in this process, the benefits of the integrated system in this part are:
- Corruptions reduction
- Monitoring the staff's functions
- Gathering all necessary information
- Providing information for other parts
- Preventing repeated observes
- Dropping unnecessary observes

D. Documentation
There has been reformation in the structure of documents and archive department like:
- Merging current archive
- Archive's classification
- Lost files reduction
- Personnel dependency reduction

E. Issuing licenses
- All this part will be done automatically through the integrated system all the rules and regulations will be applied accurately and correctly. So, there will be lot of energy and time saving.
- In calculating part in order to be fair for all the citizens all the formulas and rules and necessary parameters are common in the similar situations. And the result will be the same for similar case.
- Being parametric is a good capability of this part because as soon as the parameters changes they will be announced automatically by the integrated version to all the municipality zones
- The latest changes in taxation will be impressed fast
- The system is able to define new taxations and the way of its calculations

F. System reports
Different kinds of reports like statistic reports, managerial will be produced by the system.

G. Printing management

H. Managerial tools like:
- Organizational chart definition
- User definitions
- Users accessibility definitions
- Users functional reports
- Database manipulation
- Supporting report preparation

I. System definitions
- Parameters definitions
- Calculating parameters definition
- Cases definition
- Estate's application title definition

2-Renovation
Different parts of these are as follows:
- Fundamental information
- Estate auditing
- Owners information
- Estate location of GIS maps
- Croquis grapher
- Reports

3-Trades systems
  A.   Basic information
        a.   Jobs classification
        b.   Commercial building situation
        c.   Commercial building location
        d.   Type of ownership
        e.   Bank account
        f.   Discount table
        g.   Explanations table
  B. Auditing file formation for trades
  C. Issuing tax tickets
  D. Reports
4-Supervisors engineers
        h.   Defining the engineers identification files
        i.   Supervisor engineers allocation
        j.   Minimum of shares definitions
        k.   Connectivity to the central system
        l.   Functional reports
        m.   Functional reports of the engineering offices

9-5 Suggested plan for creating the network for implementing the urbanization integrated system in municipality of Mashed

In order to creating the proper network for implementing the urbanization integrated system in municipality of Mashed the following plans must be covered:

1.   Connectivity of the zones with central systems
2.   Central systems servers
     • DB server
     • Map server
     • Support server
     • Map support server
     • Transaction server
     • E-mail server
     • Web server
3.   Urbanization and architecture internal network
4.   Supervisor engineers interact
5.   Zones interact
6.   Internal network

7. Renovation internal network
8. Trades unit internal network
9. Revenue and income intranet
10. Execution of orders
11. Zones mayor intranet
12. Archive intranet

9-6 Characteristics of the web based urbanization integrated system

A. Applying the task follows technology

This part of the total software has had a lot of benefits and has reformed the activities of different units and their relationship with the master plan of urbanization some, of the benefits are:

- The reduction in file transmission
- Optimizing the task follow deigning for all requests
- Automatic directing the file based on its positions
- Monitoring the movement of file among units
- Preventing self opinions on files
- Staffs functional monitoring

B. Croquis grapher

This part of the system provides the possibility of drawing the estate croquis in an independent graphical environment. Through applying this sub system all the maps can be drawn by scale and the reports are printable. Since the municipality faces a large amount of the estates maps the system stores the croquis in a special format in a special database and call in them when necessary. The noticeable capabilities of the croquis grapher system are:

- Independent graphical environment
- Scale definition
- Croquis designing environment
- Defining the project characteristic
- Symbols
- Moving the objects
- Advanced graphical characteristics
- Attaching text to the croquis
- On line characteristics definition for croquis
- Printing
- Defining the printing status
- Maximizing and minimizing croquis
- Defining the characteristics of designing page

C. System map album

This album provides the possibility of storing and calling in the maps through Dwg. Dxf vectors.

The capabilities of this part are:

- Call in and callout the maps
- Turing the maps layers on and off
- Minimizing and maximizing
- Move
- Rotate
- Attaching text
- Attaching shapes and objects
- ...

D. Geographical information system

GIS is one of the most powerful software tools in the system this sub system is able to transfer the created maps or a part of it to other platforms.

E. Dynamic chart definition

F. Intelligence detailed plan functions and operations by applying the plan's map

REMARKABLE RESULTS

The effects of implementing the Web-based urbanization integrated system of municipality of Mashed with emphasis on public services can be measured through the defined indexes in the master plan of e-city of Mashed. As mentioned these indexes definitions are derived from the conceptual model of an e-city which are customized and adjusted for e-city model of Mashed. You can study the list of these indexes in chapter four. Referring to table (4-1) you can see the most important indexes in the field of e-infrastructure measurement, e-organization and e-government. These indexes are slogans which can direct and coordinate the motivations toward the goals of an organization like municipality urbanization department and causes motivation in the working environment which finally can be a proper functional index for measuring the rate of that organization success and its movement toward idol situations that is performing better and qualified public services in a municipality.

REFERENCES

1-E-government Consideration for Arab States
www.citad.org/Resources/Electronic
2-Indonesia s Roadmap to e-government
www.worldbank.org/publisector/egov/lweek/Schware.pdf
3-E-government in USA
E-government in UK
E-government in Korea
E-government in Canada
E-government in Singapore
www.ica-it.org
4-Benchmarking E-government 2002
www.unpan.org/egovernment.asp
5-E-government Strategy
www.feapmo.gov/resources/e-gov_strategy.pdf
6-Portal of US Government
www.firstgov.gov
7-Jordan s e-Government Initiative
www.unicttf-arab.org/doc/mopc.ppt
8-E-go-government Implementation The Malaysian Experience
www.kheta.ge/london/materials/national/malaysia.ppt
9-E-Government in Pakistan
www.kheta.ge/london/material/national/pakistan.ppt
10-An analysis of the IST environment in Turkey
www.isisnet.org
11-Making e Government to Government Happen
www.govis.org.nz/conference2001/judith_johnston.ppt
12-The Conceptual Framework for e-City Measurement
www.ecityforum.org.tw/shiouh_guang_wu_lecture_note.ppt
13-City of Boston
www.cityofboston.gov
14-City of Virginia Beach
www.vbgov.com

15-City of Indianapolis
www.indygov.org
16-City of Taipei
www.taipei.gov.tw
17-City of Toronto
www.city.toronto.on.ca
18-City of Watsonville
www.ci.wastonville.ca.us
19-City of Annapolis
www.annapolis.gov
20-Madison City
www.ci.medison.wi.us
21-City of Arlington
www.ci.arlington
22-City of Des Moines
www.ci.des-moines.ia.us
23-City of Grande Prairie
www.city.grande-prairie.ab.ca
24-City of Phoenix
www.ci.phoenix.az.us
25-City of Tucson
www.ci.tucson.az.us
26-City of Winnipeg
www.winnipeg.ca
27-City of Kuna
www.cityofkuna.com
28-City of Osaka
www.city.osaka.jp
29-Indian Travel Portal
www.indiantravelportal.com
30-Breken Group
www.breken.com
31-City of Chicago
www.ci.chi.il.us
32-City of Keen
www.ci.keen.nh.us
33-City of Mississauga
www.city.mississauga.on.ca

34-City of Santa Maria
www.ci.santa-maria.ca.us
35-Dubai Internet City
www.dubaiinternetcity.com
36-E-Citizen
www.ecitizen.com
37-City of Peterborough
www.epeterborough.com
38-City of Singapore
www.singaporecity.com
39-City of Kapolei
www.kapolei.com
40-City of Columbus
www.ci.columbus.oh.us
41-http://insideto.city.toronto.on.ca
Building of Information and Technology Vision for Toronto
42-IQPC Information Management for the Public Sector MAY 2002
43-City of Las Vagas.Strategic Plan 2005
44-City of San LeanardoStrategic Plan Update February 2002
45-Arianna Information Society
46-Action Plan for Information Society in Attica the Municipality of Athens Information Company
47-City of Keene Information Technology Master Plan MAY 2004
48-The e-City: Singapore Internet Case Study International Telecommunication Union APRIL 2001
49-Steven Cohen William Eimicke the Use of Internet in Government Service Delivery Columbia University FEBRUARY 2002

APPENDIX A: FIGURES

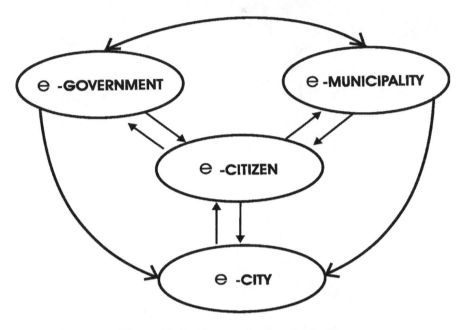

Figure (2-1): Connections and relations

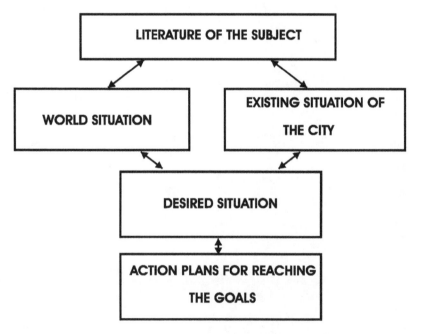

Figure (2-2): Description of methodology

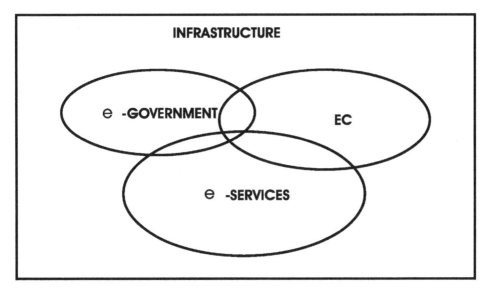

Figure (2-3): e-city model for Toronto

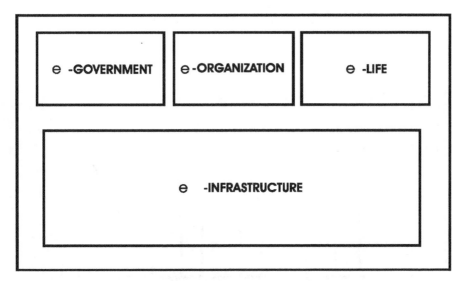

Figure (2-4): e-city model for Taipei

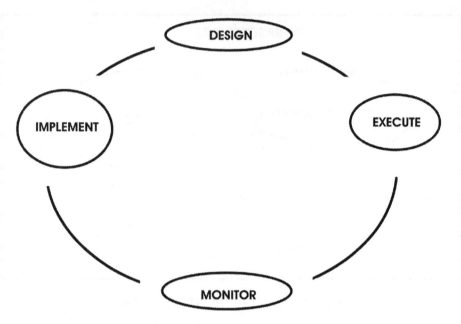

Figure (2-5): The scheme of design cycle

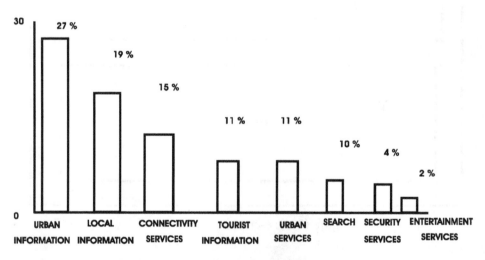

Figure (2-6): Frequency of urban services

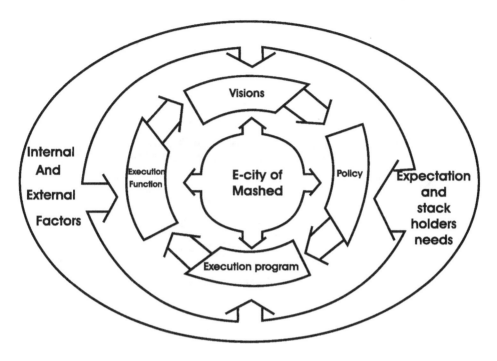

Figure (4-1): Vision, strategy, policy and plan creating cycle

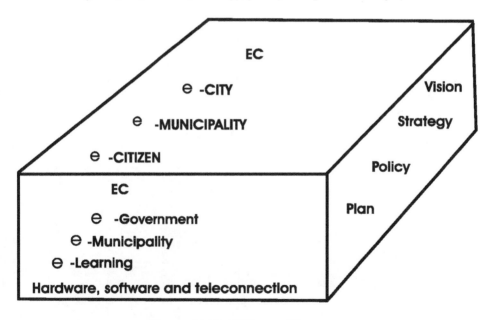

Figure (4-2): Different IT aspects

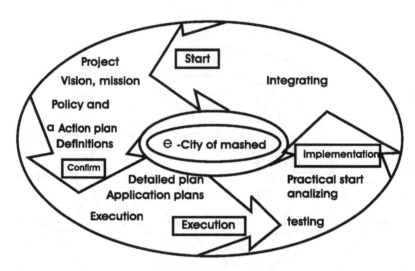

Figure (4-3): Suggested phases cycle

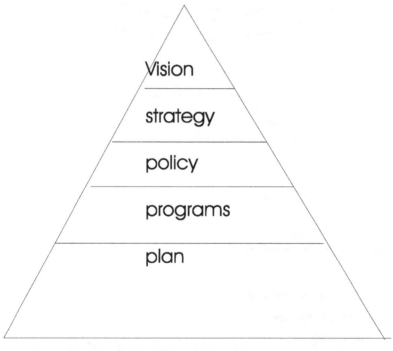

Figure (4-4): Relationship among vision, strategy, policies,
programs and plans

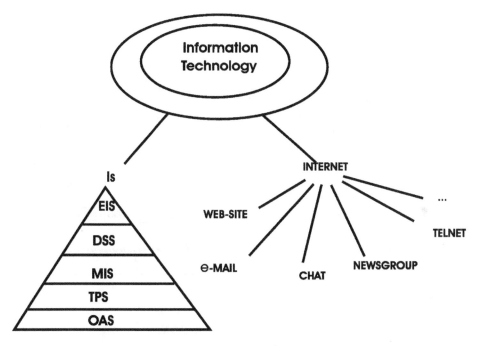

Figure (7-1): Applying IS in an organization

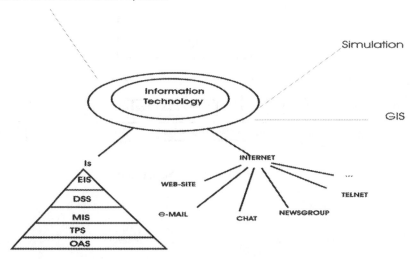

Figure (7-2): Applying IS in municipalities

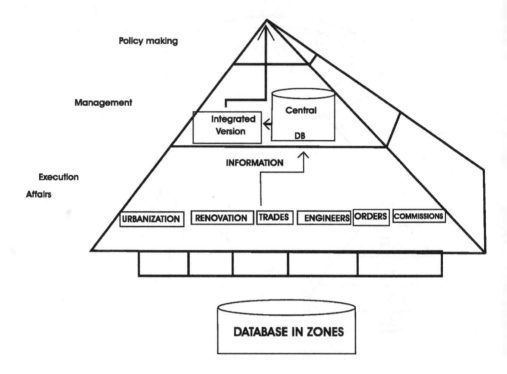

Figure (8-1): Web based urbanization integrated system

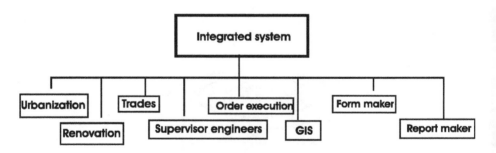

Figure (8-2): Subsystems

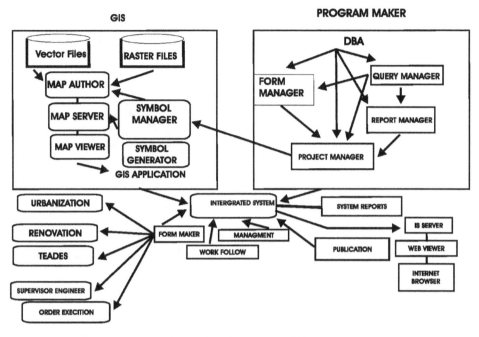

Figure (8-3): Connectivity

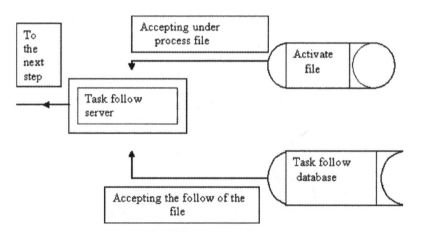

Figure (8-4): Path method for the processing file with the task
follow technology

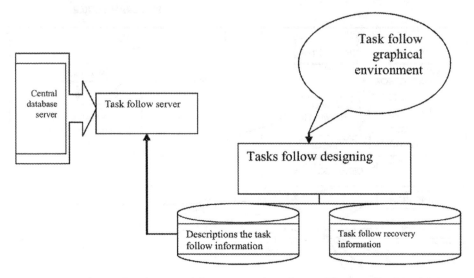

Figure (8-5): A tool for measuring the staff's function

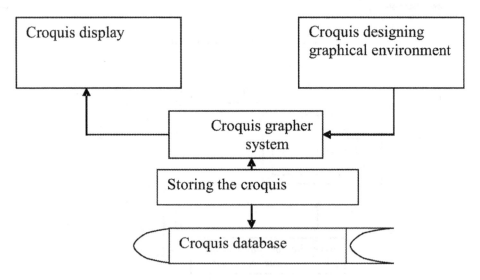

Figure (8-6): The relation among different parts of the system

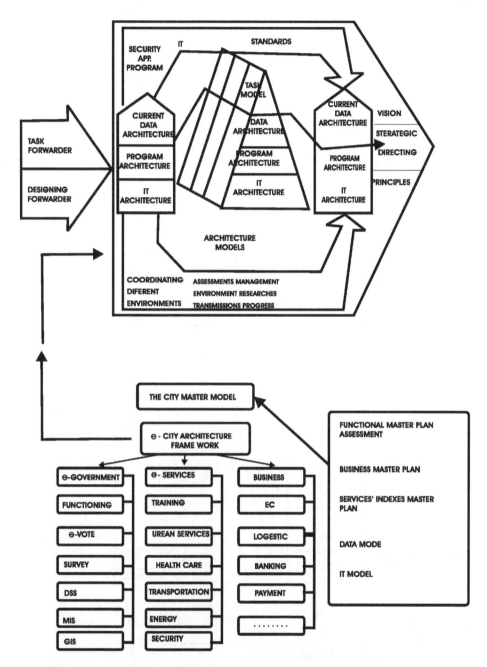

Figure (8-7): Suggested architecture frame work for e-city of Mashed

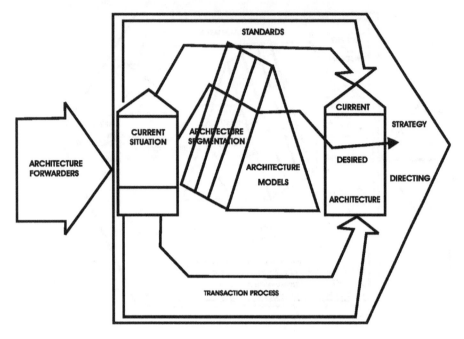

Figure (8-8): Level one

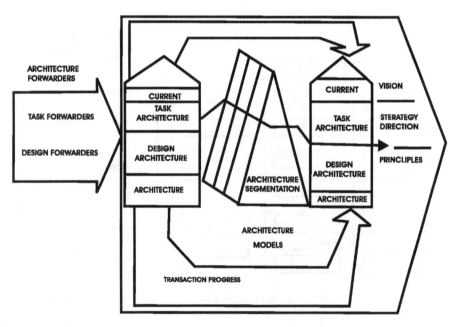

Figure (8-9): Level two

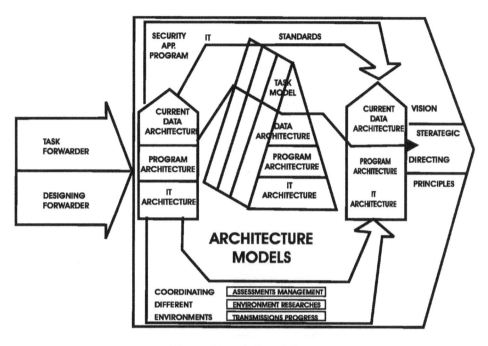

Figure (8-10): Level three

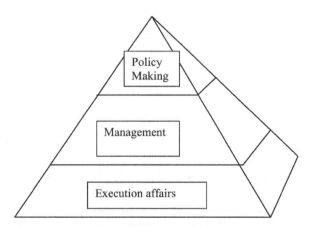

Figure (9-1): The information pyramids of municipalities can be defined in 3 levels: executive affairs, management and policy making.

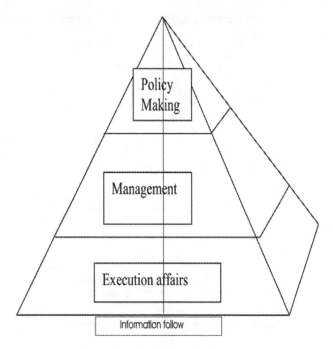

Figure (9-2): Integrated systems

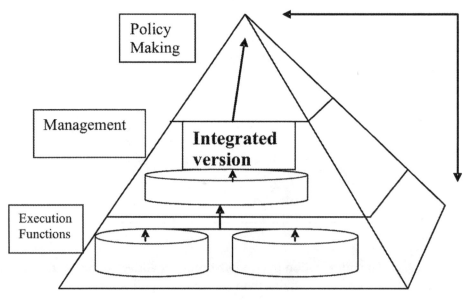

Figure (9-3): Integrated version

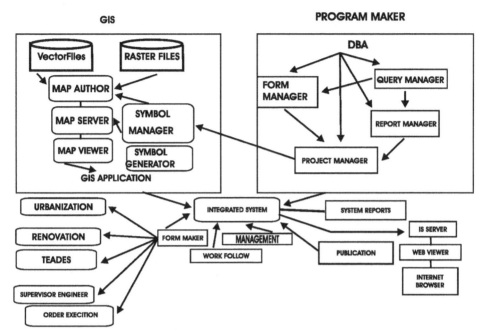

Figure (9-4): The relationships among the mentioned systems

APPENDIX B: TABLES

Development national ICT document	2003
IT international conference in Shiraz	2002
e-government research plan	2002
IT application development plan	2002
The role of IT in occupation	2001
The world internet cities conference	2001

Table (2-1): The history of IT and e-government in Iran

Strategy	Plan item	Implementation plan
1-build an information Infrastructure implementing body	1-strengthening network building	1-promotion of wide frequency network building
	2-issuing citizens with Electronic ID Strengthening network security	1-issuing of citizen's ID 2-building of an information security mechanism 3-establishment of a network emergency response team
2-universalize network educational implementing body: bureau of education	1-plan and promote a life long learning network	1-learning net 2-open cyber university
	2-increase citizen's information level	1-free three hours of internet tuition for citizens
	3-actively promoting primary and middle school information network education	1-improve school information equipment 2-on-line training for teachers
	4-establishing an electronic library	1-establishing an electronic library

3-informational government administration work implementing body: Information center	1-building of an on-line city government	1-building of city government information net 2-promotion of internet in each government body 3-promotion of official work mail boxes for section office staff 4-establishing of a city government data bank
	2-strengthening of network civil servants	1-strengthening of staff information training so that each member of staff has the ability to go—online and use the PC to handle official work
	Reassessment of organization	Promotion of residency certificate and book free service
		Revision of information center organization
4-convenient service automation implementing body: research, development and evaluation commission	1-promotion of residency certificate and book-free service	1-promotion of residency certificate and book-free service 2-applications forms on-line
	2-single window service	1-promotion of one-stop document delivery, whole process single window service
	3-provision of 24 hour service	1-promotion of various bodies service going on-line 2-telephone/fax network information service

5-citizen's nine info networks. Implementing body: information center and research, development and evaluation commission	1-free electronic mail-box	1-provision of lifelong electronic mailbox to citizens
	2-promotion of social services network	1-safety net 2-charity net 3-community net 4-medinet 5-welfare and relief net 6-establishment of neighborhood and community web-sites
	3-establishing of community computer equipment	1-wide establishment of information service stations
	4-promotion of development of leisure and tourism industry	1-culture net 2-travel net
	5-promotion of internet commerce development	1-business net 2-opening of databank for added value use

Table (2-2): The summary of the strategies, plans and their related programs

City	Virginia
Country	USA
Vision	Creating a life time society
Policies	Increasing physical, social, economical, educational life quality and qualified services for all
Strategies	Strategic thinking Increasing citizen's income Increasing useful activities Creating a positive view in people's mind Interaction and partnership Variety monitoring Proper decision making

e-services	Information for all
	Secure society
	On-line price information
	City council activities
	e-ticket
	On-line assessment
	Job information
	Job applications
	Schools and libraries
	Papers and magazines
	Contact media
	Safety points
City web-site	www.vbGov.com

Table (2-3): Virginia

City	Toronto
Country	Canada
Vision	Involving citizens in urban management
	Increasing political and managerial decision process
	New services for business men
	Increasing the rate of business in the city
	Supporting urban offices based on existing international standards
e-services	Urban transfer information
	Society events
	Health care
	Environmental
	Business licenses
	Urban tenders
	Tourists
	e-city council
	On-line job applications
	Urban rules and relations
	City events calendar
	On-line requests forms
City web-site	www.city.Tronto

Table (2-4): Toronto

City	Taipei
Country	Taiwan
Vision	Increasing internet in order to decreasing traffic Internet for all Ubiquitous life network
Policies	Increasing competition in Taipei to make it a world class city Replacing limited physical space with unlimited cyber space
e-services	Taipei GIS Taipei historical information Population information Climate information Urban transfer information Currency information Official work hour Emergency phone numbers
Related projects	e-Taiwan project Offering equal opportunity for software producers and suppliers Increasing industrial competitive and converting Taiwan into a world IT class island in Asia
City web-site	www.taipei.gov.tw

Table (2-5): Taipei

City	Indianapolis
Country	U.S.A
Vision	Excellent service to all parts of the city Facilitating ease of use of information
Policies	IT standards, IT guidelines and patterns re-engineering Reviewing IT policies Annual reviewing of budgets and IT projects Monitoring the services level Reviewing IT projects to facilitate citizen's affairs Supporting IT service providers Encouraging IT researches

e-services	On-line ticket payment On-line reporting service GIS On-line license issuing On-line purchasing e-entertainment Contact with mayor
City web-site	www.IndyGov.org

Table (2-6): Indianapolis

City	Arlington
Country	U.S.A
Vision	A world class city for life and entertainment
Policies	Involving citizen's partnership
e-services	On-line interactions GIS On-line ticket payment
	On-line tax accounting On-line city council Tourist on-line
City web-site	www.ci.Arlington.tx.us

Table (2-7): Arlington

City	Boston
Country	U.S.A
Vision	Useful content for the citizens
Policies	Educational qualification Continuous management Applied training Capacity improvement Management efficiency Upgrading lifestyle Parallelizing financial resources with city visions in the field of IT

e-services	Real estate
	City calendar
	e-voting
	My Boston
	Who am I
	Job advertisement
	City food court
	Lost and found
	My Gov
	Safety services
	Tax on-line
	Business places search
	Facilities search
	Cemeteries search
	Problem reports
	Business search
	City events
	Contact with mayor
City web-site	www.cityofBoston.gov

Table (2-8): Boston

no	city	country	vision
1	Boston	U.S.A	Useful content for the citizens
2	Virginia	U.S.A	Creating a life time society
3	Indianapolis	U.S.A	Excellent service to all parts of the city Facilitating ease of use of information
4	Taipei	TAIWAN	Increasing internet in order to decreasing traffic Internet for all Ubiquitous life network
5	Desmonies	U.S.A	Useful content for the citizens
6	Arlington	U.S.A	A world class city for life and entertainment

| 7 | Toronto | CANADA | Involving citizens in urban management Increasing political and managerial decision process New services for business men Increasing the rate of business in the city Supporting urban offices based on existing international standards |

Table (2-9): e-cities visions

no	Service title	description
1	Voting forms	Sending and receiving voting forms
2	My city	City information
3	Who ma I?	Information about the neighborhood
4	Job advertisement	Looking for job through considering the related fields
5	City food court	Reviewing monthly reports on restaurant and their ranking
6	Found and lost	Information about lost and founds things
7	My Gov	Accessing government reports through password
8	Awareness services	City events based on the interests
9	Tax	On-line tax payment
10	Ticket payment	Ticket payment
11	Animal licenses	Animal licenses
12	Searching the facilities	Libraries, parks, resorts etc
13	Average citizens age	Sending citizens' profiles to the municipality annually
14	Cemeteries search	Cemeteries search
15	Contact with city council	Counseling with the city representatives
16	Problem reports	Awaking the mayor of the city problems
17	Contact with mayor	Direct contact with mayor

no	Service title	description
18	Ticket e-payment	On-line ticket payment
19	Real estate information	Preparing equal opportunity for the citizens
20	Urban organization information	Citizen's accessing to urban official information
21	Public security information	Citizen's awareness of the security procedures
22	Environmental information	Weather and climate information
23	GIS	Receiving proper information to accessing different parts of the city easily
24	On-line purchasing	Performing pricelists
25	TV programs schedules	TV programs schedules
26	Children	On-line entertainment for kids
27	Police on-line	Putting the accidents on the show
28	Court	Information about authorizes
29	Mails' information	Following the mailed packages information
30	City transferring	Time schedules for buses and metros and routes
31	On-line tax estimation tool	Estimating taxes based on the urban rules and regulations
32	e-reservation	Ticket reservation for concerts, cinemas etc
33	Schools	Schools information
34	Libraries	Libraries information
35	On-line publishing	e-magazines and journals
36	Real estate search	Citizens access to buildings lands etc
37	Project review	Putting the reports of the process of the projects on the web
38	RFPs	Accepting RFPs on the web
39	City trends	Putting the trends information on the web
40	City calendar	City events
41	Investment opportunities and resources	Performing existing potentials for investment

no	Service title	description
42	Business search	Integrating business databases
43	Business buildings search	Searching for the best business fields
44	On-line tourist	Performing tourists interests
45	GIS	Geographical information system
46	History of the city	Separated by title
47	Population	The city population, mortality and birth rate
48	Airlines schedules	Airlines information schedules

Table (2-10): List of e-cities services

VIRGINIA	INDIANAPOLIS	ARLINGTON	TAIPEI	TORONTO	BOSTON	DOSELDORF	ESHTOTGART	SERVICE
1	2	1	4	3	3	3	4	Habitance Environment Population Geographic
3	3	1	4	6	3	4	5	City calendar Trade History Rules Municipality organizations City council transportation
1	1	1	1	1	1	2	2	Entertainment Exhibition TV programs Airlines
1	1	0	0	0	0	0	1	Games Museum Library

VIRGINIA	INDIANAPOLIS	ARLINGTON	TAIPEI	TORONTO	BOSTON	DOSELDORF	ESHTOTGART	SERVICE
4	3	2	2	0	2	2	3	On-line journals Contact with mayor Contact with city council City chat room
1	0	1	0	2	4	1	3	Real estate search Job search Business opportunity Urban facility Historical places Urban trades restaurants
3	2	0	0	0	0	0	0	Police information Contact with police Firefighting departments
1	0	2	0	1	0	4	3	Request forms for bids and trades Request forms for production Tax payment Ticket payment voting Request for identification card

Table (2-11): Frequency of the urban services in sample e-cities

Index	Country IRAN	World's ave.
Computer per 1000	5.88	10.17
Hosts per 1000	0.27	215.39
Internet access per 100	0.8	11.25
Tel. per 100	14.9	21.44
Cell phone per 100	1.51	15.3
Television per 1000	157	288.49
HR development index	0.714	0.731
Information access index	0.167	0.646
Urban population	61.6	61.9
e-government index	1.31	1.62

Table (3-1): UN indexes

field	description	index
Internet connection	Computer and internet penetration	* Cell phone rate * Internet connection rate * Band width rate * e-learning * Schools band width * Housewives' internet accessibility to internet * Public network equipment accessibility

field	description	index
Social and cultural conditions	Education	Illiteracy rate Average of public training Political freedom rate Quality of public and private schools

Human resource	Mind-workers	Ratio of IT professional to the total employees Ratio of engineers to the total employees Ratio of organization satisfaction from its IT professionals Ratio of IT training to the total employees
Rules and regulations	Reliability of on-line processing and the existing information on the network	Supporting e-privacy Preventing e-crimes
ICT infrastructure	Accessibility to the communication systems	Potential in developing telephone services Telephone per 1000 persons Cell phone per 1000 persons Web hosts per 1000 person Cost and quality of telecommunication services

field	description	index
e-services support	Portals, host, ASP, ICP support	Professional information dissemination support Software products knowledge Comparability in market
Internet connection	Network connection price list	Network equipment ownership price Organizations connection to internet price Fast accessibility to organizations Web-site creation price Intranet creation price ICT equipment investment Ratio of ICT professional to the total organization's staffs Investment on ICT training
Learning EC	EC applications programs	B2B Organization's internet programs Investment on internet Online marketing

field	description	index
Internet connecting	e-government services and management	Efficiency of application programs Online police services e-government web-site creation Wide accessibility to state organizations Internet connectivity price for the government departments Network interaction prices for governments
e-leadership	Government policy in order to up grading e-society and cooperation between public and private sectors	Governmental policy priority on ICT Investment by ICT support companies Encouraging organizations on investing on ICT Especial ICT trainings

Table (4-1): Different indexes in different fields of suggested model

Domain & domain's NO.		Sub-domain NO.		Plan's NO.	
D	7	0	3	0	4

Table (4-2)

#	Domain's name: organization's program rules and regulations	Domain's code
	Plan's name	Plan's code
1	ICT strategic councils in e-city of MASHED	D40100
2	IT organization of MASHED	D40200
3	Providing definitions for key processes in the city	D40300
4	re-engineering and reviewing the urban processes	D40400

Table (4-3): Suggested plans in the field of organization's programs, rules and regulations

#	Domain's name: financial resources	Domain's code: D5
	Plan's name	Plan's code
1	Absorbing financial resources from TAKFA	D50100
2	Absorbing financial resources from states budgets	D50200
3	Local credits for the e-city projects	D50300
4	Donator's support	D50400
5	International bank support	D50500
6	Private sector investment	D50600
7	Organization's credits	D50700
8	Foreign investment	D50800
9	NGO's support	D50900
10	Interior ministry support	D51000
11	Partnership support	D51200
12	Applying advertisement for increasing the city's income	D51300
13	Encouraging people for consecration	

Table (4-4): Financial developments

Program code	program	system	Sub-system	code
D6	System field	Integrated office system (D601)	Financial	D60101
			Personnel	D60102
			Call out	D60103
			Wage	D60104
			Facility	D60105
			Paperless	D60106
			Security	D60107
			Insurance	D60108
			Selection	D60109
			Properties	D60110
			Warehouse	D60111
			Budget	D60112

		Integrated e-services system(D602)	Blockade	D60201
			Machinery system	D60202
			Recycle system	D60203
			Cemetery system	D60204
			Fire fighting	D60205
			Greengrocers	D60206
			Green space	D60207
		EC-system (D603)	Auction	D60301
			Sales	D60302
			Purchase	D60303
			Trends	D60304
			Bid	D60305
		Urbanization integrated system (604)	Fraternity	D60401
			Revenue	D60402
			renovation	D60403
			Supervisor engineer	D60404
			Execution of orders	D60405
			Commissions	D60406
			Urban light train	D60500
			Tax accounting	D60600
			Ticket payment	D60700
			Traffic	D60800
			Transmission	D60900
			Taxi	D61000

				Bus	D61100
				Vehicle tariff	D61200
				Archive	D61300
				Project control	D61400
				Training	D61500
				Real estate	D61600
				Integrated library	D61800
				MIS	D61900
				Contractors	D62000
				Inter organizational communications	D62100
				GIS	D62200

Table (4-5): Suggested systems

System's name	Office automation system
Code	D601
Description	This system is consist of : accounting, personnel, call out, payment, facilities, paperless, security, insurance, assessment, warehouse and budget which will mechanize all the organization's internal activities
Characteristics	Work follow Office management Ease of processes Dynamic reporting system Form designing Work follow definition Security levels definition Web-based system
Users	All the municipality zones and departments and official organizations
System's name	Urban services

Code	D602
Description	The sub systems : blockade, machinery, recycle, cemetery, firefighting, parks and green spaces and GIS
Characteristics	Dynamic reporting Form designing Security levels definitions
Users	Municipality and its deputies and departments
System's name	Electronic commerce
Code	D603
Description	The sub systems are: sale, trade, bid, auction
Characteristics	Public friendly
Users	People, official organizations, municipality departments, trades
System's name	Urbanization
Code	D604
Description	The sub systems are: revenue, renovation, estate, supervisor engineers, orders execution and GIS
Characteristics	Dynamic reporting Form designing Work follow definition Security level definition Parametric ticket accounting
Users	Municipalities as the main users and trades and citizens as peripheral users
System's name	Light train
Code	D60500
Description	Controlling and monitoring the light trains in order to perform better services
System's name	Taxation
Code	D60600
Description	Recording the assessment information of the citizens, accounting the taxes amount, connection to the office integrated system, defining the level of accessibility to the system
Users	System users

System's name	Ticket payment
Code	D60700
Description	Accepting the tickets from info kiosks
Users	The public
System's name	Traffic control
Code	D60800
Description	Traffic management, travelers information, public transportation, critic management, security
Users	The organization of traffic control
System's name	Public transportation
Code	D60900
Description	Recording the arrival and departure information of the buses
Users	The public transportation organization
System's name	Urban transportation
Code	D61100
Description	Recording the urban buses to the parking and garages, controlling the buses in their paths, recording the buses identifications, complaints controlling and GPS
Users	The urban transportation organization and citizens
System's name	Vehicle taxation and tariff system
Code	D61200
Description	Recording the vehicle information and issuing tax tickets etc
Users	Different zones of the municipality
System's name	Archive and documentation
Code	D61300
Description	Defining the accessibility level to the documents, creating databases of documents, searching system
Users	Different zones of the municipality and the official organizations
System's name	Project management
Code	D61400

Description	Recording the project management information and resources, controlling the resources, project improvement, preparing the managerial reports for decision making, contacting to contractors
Users	Municipality departments
System's name	Training and education
Description	Recording the trainers and the trainees information and the courses
Users	Municipality departments and companies with more than 30 personnel
System's name	Estate system
Code	D61600
Description	Creating estate database
Users	Citizens and the municipality zones
System's name	Streets appellation
Code	D61700
Description	Preparing the streets identifications
Users	The municipality public affairs and zones
System's name	Integrated library
Code	D61800
Description	Recording all libraries information, connecting them, searching and membership
Users	citizens
System's name	MIS
Code	D61900
Description	Preparing necessary statistics reports for management and databases, assessing them and defining the accessibility levels
Users	Municipalities and their departments
System's name	Contractor's system
Code	D62000
Description	Contractors affairs, recording their information, contacting to the project control system

Users	Municipalities zones and related organizations
System's name	Organizational interactions
Code	D62100
Description	A connection bridge among the different organizations of the city and their interactions
Users	Municipalities, companies and official organizations
System's name	GIS
Code	D62200
Description	Accessibility to the maps and geographic information, creating maps databases, recording the geographical information and locations, connectivity to urbanization system, accessibility definitions and classification of geographical information
Users	Municipalities, related organizations, companies and public

Table (4-6): Detailed definition of the systems

Program code	Program	Plan	Sub-plan	Plan's code
D7	Information dissemination field	Cultural services (D701)	Online cultural centers	D70101
			Online publication	D70102
			Online TV	D70103
			Online cultural information	D70104
			Online entertainment	D70105
		Tourism (D702)	Online tourist	D70200
			Historical places	D70301
			Municipality online	D70302

		Urban infor- mation dissemi- nation (D703)	Urban information	D70303
			Business information	D70304
			Trades information	D70305
			Official organization information	D70306
		Urban connec- tivity (D704)	Municipality on-line	D70401
			City council	D70402
			City on-line	D70403
		Safety and security (D705)	Police on-line	D70501
			Firefighting	D70502
			Health care	D70503
		Urban transpor- tation (D706)	Online transportation services	D70601
			Inter cities trips on- line services	D70602

Table (4-7): Related programs

Plan's name : on-line cultural centers
Plan's target : creating an on-line DB
Plan's range : cultural centers of the city Cultural centers programs Cinema and theater Ticket reservation
Plan's duties : creating a powerful DB

Prerequisite : information dissemination companies identity Benchmarking Feasibility study of the existing systems
Benefits for the city: municipality management development
Benefits for the citizens: Easy accessibility Time and cost saving
Undertaker : municipality
Teammate : Cultural centers
Plan's name : On-line publishing
Plan's target : Creating a publication DB
Plan's range: Mashed's journals Mashed's daily papers The city publications On-line delivery
Plan's duties : Creating powerful DBs
Prerequisite : Papers and magazines recognition Benchmarking the best patterns Feasibility of the existing systems
Benefits for the city: More income for the city
Benefits for the citizens: 24/7 accessibility Easy access Time and cost saving People's awareness
Undertaker : municipality
Teammate : publication companies

Plan's name : TV and radio on-line
Plan's target : On-line programs
Plan's range : Radio information TV information
Plan's duties : Creating powerful systems and networks
Prerequisite : Identity of on-line systems Identity of the necessary infrastructure Benchmarking Feasibility of the existing systems
Benefits for the city: World accessibility to the city TV and radio programs
Benefits for the citizens: On-line access
Undertaker :municipality
Teammate : radio and TV organization
Plan's name : On-line cultural information
Plan's target : Creating DB
Plan's range : Customs information Historical information
Plan's duties : Creating related DB
Prerequisite …
Benefits for the city: Tourist attraction
Benefits for the citizens: Peoples awareness attraction
Undertaker : Municipality

Teammate :Islamic culture organization
Plan's name : City spots on-line
Plan's target : Performing necessary information
Plan's range: City spots Urban facility spots Training and education spots Business centers Cultural centers Health care centers Sport spots Religious spots
Plan's duties : More and easy accessibility to different spots of the city
Prerequisite : City DB
Benefits for the city: City development and better planning for the city
Benefits for the citizens: Easy accessing to the city locations and spots
Undertaker : Municipality
Teammate : Both public and private sector
Plan's name :on-line municipality
Plan's target : Citizen's accessibility to the municipality information and increasing citizen's partnership and highlighting the municipality's capabilities
Plan's range : Municipality and all its departments and zones and staffs and management
Plan's duties : Performing the newest programs and decisions or rules and regulations
Prerequisite : Preparing necessary documentation

Benefits for the city: Reduction on the number of the citizens' trips to municipality
Benefits for the citizens: Up to date information
Undertaker : Municipality
Teammate : Municipality organizations
Plan's name : On-line urban information
Plan's target : Performing necessary information about public situations
Plan's range : City managers City representatives City map History City calendar Weather and climate Environment Found and lost properties City statistics reports
Plan's duties : Information classification Information updates search
Prerequisite : Feasibility study and priority definition
Benefits for the city: Stability of the city situation as an information base
Benefits for the citizens: More and easy accessibility
Undertaker : Municipality
Teammate : Private sector
Plan's name : On-line business information

Plan's target :   Electronic commerce development
Plan's range :   Trends, bids, auctions, stock markets …
Plan's duties :   Easy accessibility to business information
Prerequisite :   Databases
Benefits for the city: More investment and partnership and income
Benefits for the citizens: Easy and safe business
Undertaker :   Municipality
Teammate :   Companies and stock markets
Plan's name :official organizations
Plan's target :   Easy and fast accessibility to the official organizations
Plan's range :   All the governmental organization
Plan's duties :   Performing a powerful search engine
Prerequisite :   Creating DB for the governmental organizations
Benefits for the city: …
Benefits for the citizens: Time and cost saving   More awareness
Undertaker :   Municipality
Teammate :   Governmental organizations
Plan's name :   On-line city council
Plan's target :   Interaction between the city council and citizens

Plan's range :   City council
Plan's duties :   interaction
Prerequisite :   Accurate time scheduling of the city council representatives
Benefits for the city: Better decision making process   Fast and wide interaction with citizens
Benefits for the citizens: Effective planning
Undertaker :   Municipality
Teammate :   City council
Plan's name :police on-line
Plan's target :   Creating police DB
Plan's range :   Police information   Security   Rules and regulation
Plan's duties :   Creating powerful database
Prerequisite :   ….
Benefits for the city: Insecurity reduction
Benefits for the citizens: Safer society
Undertaker :   Municipality
Teammate :   police
Plan's name :   Health on-line
Plan's target :   Creating health care DB

| Plan's range : |
| Emergency departments and health monitoring stations |
| **Plan's duties :** |
| Creating a powerful network |
| **Benefits for the city:** |
| A happy and healthy city |
| **Benefits for the citizens:** |
| Healthy citizens and 24/7 accessibility to the medical services |
| **Undertaker :municipality** |
| **Teammate :health care centers** |

Table (4-8): The plans of electronic city of Mashed

Goal / Vision		upgrading urbanization indexes	Improvement the urban environment	Improving the urban transportation	Urban security	Cultural affairs	Increasing partnership	Encouraging the culture of control	Upgrading social and cultural affairs	Reforming the official and final structure	Establishing coordinating in the management system
e-government vision	Knowledge base economy										
	Creating information society										
	Qualified life										
e-city vision	Better services										
	A world class city										
	Competitive environment										
	Traffic reduction										

Goal Vision		upgrading urbanization indexes	Improvement the urban environment	Improving the urban transportation	Urban security	Cultural affairs	Increasing partnership	Encouraging the culture of control	Upgrading social and cultural affairs	Reforming the official and final structure	Establishing coordinating in the management system
Municipality vision	Citizen oriented management										
	24/7 services										
	Quality guarantee of services										
	Sustainable revenue										
	Process clarification										
e-citizen vision	Information society citizen										

Table (4-9): The relation between current and future urban goals and the vision of e-city of Mashed

Domain		Infrastructure	hardware	Training	Rules and regulation	Financial resources
Vision	Code	D1	D2	D3	D4	D5
e-government vision	Knowledge oriented economy			*		*
e-government vision	Creating information society	*			*	
e-government vision	Qualified life			*	*	
e-city vision	Better services	*	*			
e-city vision	A world class city	*	*		*	
e-city vision	Competitive environment		*		*	*
e-city vision	Traffic reduction			*	*	
Municipality vision	Citizen oriented in management			*		
Municipality vision	24/7 services	*	*		*	
Municipality vision	Quality guarantee of services		*		*	
Municipality vision	Sustainable revenue					*
Municipality vision	Process clarification				*	
e-citizen vision	Information society citizen			*		

Table (4-10): The matrix of relations between domains and visions in e-city of Mashed

Strategies / Domains	Information infrastructure development	Intelligent supervision on urban services upgrading	Training the citizens about e-services	Integrating the systems	more revenue for the city by applying IT	Reviewing the current procedures and improving them	Upgrading the quality, the services, the staffs and training	Creating urban databases
Infrastructure	*							
Hardware	*							
Training	*	*	*					*
Rules and regulations		*		*		*	*	
Financial resources		*			*			*
systems		*		*		*	*	
Cultural services	*	*					*	
Tourism	*	*					*	
Urban information dissemination	*	*					*	
Safety services	*	*					*	
Urban transmission		*					*	
Urban connectivity	*	*					*	

Table (4-11): The matrix of domains and strategies in e-city of Mashed

Domain		Cultural services					tourism	Urban information						Urban connectivity services			Safety services			Urban transportation	
Plan		Cultural center	publications	Radio and TV	Cultural information	On-line entertainment	On-line tourism	Urban spots	Online municipality	City on-line	Business information	Trades on-line	Governmental organization	Online municipality	City council on-line	City on-line	Police on-line	Firefighting	Online health care	Urban transportation	Inter cities transportation
vision \ code		D70101	D70102	D70103	D70104	D70105	D70200	D70301	D70302	D70303	D70304	D70305	D70306	D70401	D70402	D70403	D70501	D70502	D70503	D70601	D70602
e-government vision	Knowledge oriented economy					*	*													*	*
	Creating information society	*	*	*	*	*	*	*	*	*	*	*	*	*	*	*~	*	*	*	*	*
	Qualified life	*	*	*	*	*							*	*	*	*	*	*	*	*	*
e-city vision	Better services	*	*	*	*	*											*	*	*	*	*
	A world class city	*	*	*	*	*			*								*	*	*	*	*
	Competitive environment						*				*										
	Traffic reduction	*	*			*		*	*	*	*	*	*	*	*	*					

Domain		Cultural services					tourism	Urban information						Urban connectivity services			Safety services		Urban transportation	
Plan		Cultural center	publications	Radio and TV	Cultural information	On-line entertainment	On-line tourism	Urban spots	Online municipality	City on-line	Business information	Trades on-line	Governmental organization	Online municipality	City council on-line	City on-line	Police on-line	Firefighting	Online health care	Urban transportation	Inter cities transportation
code \ vision		D70101	D70102	D70103	D70104	D70105	D70200	D70301	D70302	D70303	D70304	D70305	D70306	D70401	D70402	D70403	D70501	D70502	D70503	D70601	D70602
Municipality vision	Citizen oriented in management												*	*							
	24/7 services												*	*	*						
	Quality guarantee of services																				
	Sustainable revenue																				
	Process clarification												*	*	*						
e-citizen vision	Information society citizen																				

Table (4-12): The matrix of domains and visions in e-city of Mashed, information domain

Plan's domain	Code	e-government vision			e-city vision		
		Knowledge oriented economy	Creating information society	Qualified life	Better services	A world class city	Competitive environment
GIS	D62000		*				
MIS	D61900		*				
Integrated library	D61800	*	*				
Real estate	D61600		*		*		
Training	D61500	*	*		*		
Project control	D61400		*				
Documentation	D61300		*				
Tariff	D61200		*		*		
Transportation	D60900		*		*		
Traffic control	D60800		*		*		
Ticket payment	D60700		*		*		
Taxation	D60600		*				
Light train system	D60500		*		*		
Urbanization system	D60400			*	*		
Electronic commerce	D60300	*	*	*	*	*	*
Urban services	D60200	*	*		*		
Integrated official system	D60100		*				

	Competitive environment																
	Traffic reduction			*			*	*									
e-municipality vision	Citizen oriented in management																
	24/7 services	*		*				*	*	*	*				*	*	
	Quality guarantee of services	*	*	*	*	*	*	*	*	*	*	*	*	*	*	*	*
	Sustainable revenue		*														
	Process clarification	*	*	*	*	*	*	*	*	*	*	*	*	*	*	*	*
e-citizen vision	Information society citizen																

Table (4-13): The matrix of domains and visions in e-city of Mashed, system domain

Macro plans	Public sector (billion rials)	Private sector's share
ICT development	120.2	50%
e-government	10.8	20%
e-learning	9.6	30%
e-healthcare	9.2	60%
EC	14.4	80%
Post development	1.5	20%
Sum of credits	174.7	

Table (5-1): ICT credit allocation

Macro plans	Public sector (billion rials)	Private sector's share
ICT development	5	50%
e-government	0.415	20%
e-learning	0.37	30%
e-healthcare	0.354	60%
EC	0.554	80%
Post development	0.58	20%
Sum of credits from the countries ICT budget	6.75	

Table (5-2): Predicted table

978-0-595-45738-0
0-595-45738-X

www.ingramcontent.com/pod-product-compliance
Lightning Source LLC
Chambersburg PA
CBHW051233050326

40689CB00007B/915